D1003716

A CHALLENGE

TO THE

NEW PERSPECTIVE

REVISITING PAUL'S DOCTRINE OF JUSTIFICATION

*With an essay
by Donald A. Hagner*

PETER STUHLMACHER

InterVarsity Press
Downers Grove, Illinois

InterVarsity Press
P.O. Box 1400, Downers Grove, IL 60515-1426
World Wide Web: www.ivpress.com
E-mail: mail@ivpress.com

InterVarsity Press® is the book-publishing division of InterVarsity Christian Fellowship/USA®, a student movement active on campus at hundreds of universities, colleges and schools of nursing in the United States of America, and a member movement of the International Fellowship of Evangelical Students. For information about local and regional activities, write Public Relations Dept., InterVarsity Christian Fellowship/USA, 6400 Schroeder Rd., P.O. Box 7895, Madison, WI 53707-7895.

All Scripture quotations, unless otherwise indicated, are the author's own translation.

The original edition of "Paul and Judaism: Testing the New Perspective" by Donald A. Hagner was published in Bulletin for Biblical Research 3 *(1993): 111-30.*

ISBN 0-8308-2661-0

Printed in the United States of America ∞

Library of Congress Cataloging-in-Publication Data

Stuhlmacher, Peter.
    Revisiting Paul's doctrine of justification: a challenge to the new perspective/Peter
Stuhlmacher; with an essay by Donald A. Hagner.
        p. cm.
    Includes bibliographical references.
    ISBN 0-8308-2661-0 (paper: alk. paper)
    1. Justification—Biblical teaching. 2. Bible. N.T. Epistles of Paul—Theology. 3.
Justification—History of doctrines—20th century. 4. Bible. N.T. Epistles of
    Paul—Criticism, interpretation, etc.—History—20th century. I. Title.
BS2655.J8 S78 2001
234'.7'09—dc21   2001026463

25 24 23 22 21 20 19 18 17 16 15 14 13 12 11 10 9 8 7 6 5 4 3 2 1

21 20 19 18 17 16 15 14 13 12 11 10 09 08 07 06 05 04 03 02 01

Contents

Abbreviations

BBR	*Bulletin for Biblical Research*
Bib	*Biblica*
BJRL	*Bulletin of the John Rylands University Library of Manchester*
CBQ	*Catholic Biblical Quarterly*
ConBNT	Coniectanea Biblica Neotestamentica
CTJ	*Calvin Theological Journal*
ET	English Translation
EvQ	*Evangelical Quarterly*
HJ	*Hibbert Journal*
HTR	*Harvard Theological Review*
Int	*Interpretation*
JETS	*Journal of the Evangelical Theological Society*
JBL	*Journal of Biblical Literature*
JQR	*Jewish Quarterly Review*
JSJ	*Journal for the Study of Judaism in the Persian, Hellenistic and Roman Period*
JSNT	*Journal for the Study of the New Testament*
JSNTSS	*Journal for the Study of the New Testament* Supplement Series
JSOT	*Journal for the Study of the Old Testament*
JSOTSS	*Journal for the Study of the Old Testament* Supplement Series
JTS	*Journal of Theological Studies*
NJB	New Jerusalem Bible
NovT	*Novum Testamentum*
NovTSup	Supplement to *Novum Testamentum*
NRSV	New Revised Standard Version
NTS	*New Testament Studies*
RestQ	*Restoration Quarterly*

SBLDS	Society of Biblical Literature Dissertation Series
SEÅ	*Svensk Exegetisk Årsbok*
SJT	*Scottish Journal of Theology*
SNTSMS	Society for New Testament Studies Monograph Series
SSEJC	*Studies in Early Judaism and Christianity*
TB	Theologische Bücherei
USQR	*Union Seminary Quarterly Review*
WA	*World Archaeology*
WTJ	*Westminster Theological Journal*
WUNT	Wissenschaftliche Untersuchungen zum Neuen Testament
ZAW	Zeitschrift für die Alttestamentliche Wissenschaft
1QpHab	*Pesher Habakkuk*
1QS	*Serek Hayahad* or *Rule of the Community*
4QMMT[e]	*Miqsat Ma'ase ha-Torah*[e]
4Q398	4QHalakhic Letter[e]

Preface

In spring 2000 I delivered the eleventh annual Biblical Studies Lectures as a guest of Beeson Divinity School, Birmingham, Alabama, on the Pauline doctrine of justification. I was also invited by the Southern Baptist Theological Seminary, Louisville, Kentucky, to give the Annual Gheens Lectures on the same theme. I am grateful to both institutions for their overwhelming hospitality, and I would also like to thank Daniel P. Bailey, Ph.D., for translating my German manuscripts into readable English.

The subject matter gave me a new opportunity to discuss publicly the Pauline doctrine of justification. Having been occupied in recent years with the nature of early Christian mission and with Paul's eschatology, the time seemed ripe for a corrective of the historical and theological one-sidedness of the "new perspective on Paul" developed by Krister Stendahl, Ed Parish Sanders and James D. G. Dunn. Reading the letters of the apostle, one sees that his doctrine of justification belongs in the context of the apostolic mission to Jews and Gentiles, which was shaped by the expectation of the kingdom of God.

My friend Don Hagner has already pointed out some of the weaknesses of the new perspective in his article "Paul and Judaism—The Jewish Matrix of Early Christianity: Issues in the Current Debate," *Bulletin for Biblical Research* 3 (1993): 111-30. The article is reproduced here in an updated form.

Hagner and I are convinced that Paul's doctrine of justification should no longer remain obscured by the false understanding argued for by William Wrede and Albert Schweitzer, that it was simply a polemical doctrine formulated against Judaizers, which was of minor importance compared to the mystical salvation taught by the apostle. This view has been revived by some representatives of the new perspective. But the so-called mysticism of the apostle is an implication of his concept of the atonement: God made Christ "for our sake . . . to be sin who knew no sin, so that in him we might become the righteousness of God" (2 Cor 5:21); Christ's sacrificial death on the cross of Golgotha is the forensic basis provided by God for the justification of the ungodly by faith in Christ alone. This justification is concerned with the survival of Jews and Gentiles in front of God's throne of judgment at the end of time. This final judgment lies in the hands of Jesus Christ and leads to the establishment of the kingdom of God over the whole of the new creation.

Peter Stuhlmacher
Tübingen, August 2000

PRELIMINARY REMARKS

The Christian Bible consisting of Old and New Testaments has not been handed down to us in order that we might seek out only those stories and sayings that impress us and then leave the rest or even dismiss it. Instead we should think through this two-part book and ponder its texts until we discover that the one God who created the world and chose Israel to be his own people speaks to us through the biblical writings and had our salvation in mind while we were still "weak" and "sinners," or even before we were in the world (cf. Rom 5:6-8).

One of Bible's essential themes is justification. When we read Paul's letter to the Christians in Rome, we see that for the apostle the gospel of God concerning Jesus Christ (cf. Rom 1:1-4) is the gospel of the justification of sinners by faith alone for Christ's sake. According to Romans 1:16-17, the righteousness of God is revealed in the gospel to everyone who believes. This revelation goes first to the Jew but also to the Greek (Gentile), and it is in keeping with the word of God from Habakkuk 2:4: "The one who is righteous by faith shall live." Paul confesses this gospel of God's righteousness, and he goes on to declare to his Roman audience what is involved in the righteousness of God as revealed in the gospel. As Adolf Schlatter has correctly seen, "God's righteousness" or *Gottes Gerechtigkeit* (the title of Schlatter's Romans commentary[1]) is the theme of the entire letter to the Romans.

In the lectures that I have been invited to give, I would like us to concentrate upon the theme of justification. But before we do so, we must be clear about two things. First, this is a challenging theme. It was not disputed only in Paul's time but remains controversial today. Therefore, we will have to make a historical effort to delve into the questions about justification. And we will not be able to avoid taking a position in the controversy over it.

This first lecture is an introduction to the conceptual world and historical background of Paul's proclamation of justification. The second is devoted to the missionary perspective from which Paul saw justification, while the third lecture deals with the content of his doctrine of justification.

---

[1]Compare Adolf Schlatter, *Gottes Gerechtigkeit—Ein Kommentar zum Römerbrief* (1935; reprint, Stuttgart: Calwer Verlag, 1952); ET: Adolf Schlatter, *Romans: The Righteousness of God*, trans. Siegfried S. Schatzmann (Peabody, Mass.: Hendrickson, 1995).

One

THE GOSPEL OF GOD'S RIGHTEOUSNESS

Paul wrote the letter to the Romans as a converted Jew. More precisely, the risen Christ granted him "grace and apostleship" so that he might "bring about the obedience of faith among all the Gentiles," including the people in Rome (cf. Rom 1:5-6). Prior to his conversion the apostle belonged to the Pharisees, who were committed to the law, and he had learned in the school of Rabbi Gamaliel I in Jerusalem to work with the holy Scriptures and the doctrines of the Jewish faith (cf. Acts 22:3). Therefore he had a precise knowledge of the Hebrew and Greek Bibles as well as the faith traditions of ancient Judaism. He presupposes a knowledge of the Mosaic law even among his addressees in Rome (cf. Rom 7:1). Presumably some of them came from the group of the so-called godfearers, who gathered at every Jewish synagogue in the Diaspora. They avoided circumcision, but were religiously interested in the Jewish doctrine of the one God and his will, and they knew the law and the prophets as well as the traditional Jewish prayers and confessions from the synagogue service.

For us, these circumstances mean that we have before us in Romans some statements that the apostle and the original recipients of the letter understood well (perhaps right away), but that become transparent to us only once we have clarified the background from which the apostle starts. That is especially true for the doctrine of justification. Paul sharpens this doctrine into a message about the *justification of the ungodly*: Abraham is for Paul "our forefather," who was the first to believe in the one God "who justifies the ungodly," and this faith "was reckoned to him as righteousness" according to Genesis 15:6 (cf. Rom 4:1-5). Moreover, in his mission from God, Christ died "for the ungodly" while we were still weak and in our sins (cf. Rom 5:6-8). Though we can make sense of these statements on our own, they gain a sharper profile when we examine the traditional milieu from which they come and ask how they are to be understood against this background.

1. Justification as an End-Time Act of Judgment

If we wish to understand the Pauline doctrine of justification, we must first consider that justification involves an *act of judgment*. Justification is decidedly located in the final judgment. As passages such as Zechariah 14, Joel 3, Malachi 4, the so-called Isaiah Apocalypse in Isaiah 24—27, and Daniel 7 and 12:1-4 show, Israel and the nations are heading for an end-time *judgment of God's wrath* according to the Old Testament Jewish expectation. Only the saved community of God's elect will emerge from this judgment purified. The pre-Christian Qumran texts speak about the triumph of God and of the archangel Michael over the powers of Belial and about the rising of the "sun of righteousness" over the saved community of Israel and the cosmos as a whole

(cf. 1Q27 1:6-7 with Mal 4:2). According to the Essenes of Qumran, the pious cannot achieve acquittal in the judgment by their
own perfection either now or in the future. Rather, they are
dependent on the mercy of almighty God. Hence in a style
anticipating Paul, the supplicant in 1QS 11:10-15 affirms:

> For mankind has no way,
>   and man is unable to establish his steps
> since justification is with God
>   and perfection of way is out of His hand.
> All things come to pass by His knowledge;
> He establishes all things by His design
>   and without Him nothing is done.
>
> As for me,
>   if I stumble, the mercies of God
>   shall be my eternal salvation.
> If I stagger because of the sin of the flesh,
>   my justification shall be
>   by the righteousness of God which endures for ever.
> When my distress is unleashed
>   He will deliver my soul from the Pit
>   and will direct my steps to the way.
> He will draw me near by His grace,
>   and by His mercy will He bring my justification.
> He will judge me in the righteousness of His truth
>   and in the greatness of His goodness
>   He will pardon all my sins.
> Through His righteousness He will cleanse me
>   of the uncleanness of man
>   and of the sins of the children of men,
> that I may confess to God His righteousness,
>   and His majesty to the Most High.[1]

---

[1]Geza Vermes, trans., *The Dead Sea Scrolls in English*, 3rd ed. (London: Penguin,
1987), pp. 79-80.

In the Ezra Apocalypse (4 Ezra, or 2 Esdras in the NRSV) written at the end of the first century A.D., there is a similar confession:

> For in truth there is no one among those who have been born who has not acted wickedly; among those who have existed there is no one who has not done wrong. For in this, O Lord, your righteousness and goodness will be declared, when you are merciful to those who have no store of good works. (4 Ezra 8:35-36)

Yet in spite of this confession, 4 Ezra speaks of a final judgment in which God's mercy and patience will no longer have any effect. Instead, "righteous deeds shall awake, and unrighteous deeds shall not sleep" (7:35). Reward awaits good works, while retribution awaits evil works, and only a few men and women obtain access to the "place of rest" (*locus requietionis,* 7:36). They are the ones who have been victorious in the struggle for a life lived according to the precepts of the Mosaic law (cf. 7:33-38 with 7:70-74, 127-31). For the godless (wicked) there is no mercy, according to 4 Ezra.

2. The Idea of Justification

Behind the *idea of justification* stands a long process of working out this tradition in Israel and early Judaism. According to Ezekiel 18, people stand or fall before God as individuals on the basis of their own righteous or wicked deeds. Although, according to popular Jewish wisdom, righteousness leads to welfare and respect while unrighteousness leads to affliction and sickness, the book of Job establishes that even a man beset by nothing but disaster can be righteous in God's eyes and "justified": Job not only insisted in the existence of his heavenly advocate and savior (cf. Job 16:19; 19:25-27), he also was allowed to hear and see him (cf. 42:5). After having acknowledged his human inability to understand the wonderful counsel of the almighty God and his repentance "in dust and ashes," Job is vindicated by this God over against his friends, so that they have to offer a burnt offering for themselves while Job intercedes for them with his prayer (cf. 42:7-9).

Individual Jewish sinners learn through penitential prayers such as Psalm 51 to acknowledge and confess their sins and to ask God for forgiveness. From Second Isaiah onwards, all of history acquires for Israel a judicial character. God stands by his servant Israel in the legal case with opponents and accusers among the peoples, and helps to vindicate Israel (cf. Is 50:7-9). By virtue of the righteousness that proceeds from God, Israel will be established in salvation (cf. Is 54:14, 17). At the same time, according to the song of the Suffering Servant (Is 52:13—53:12), the chosen servant of God helps "the many" before God to obtain a new right to their existence by his innocent vicarious suffering. He does so by giving up his own life in death as an אָשָׁם, that is, a way of "wiping out guilt,"[2] and also by interceding for them. "The many" here are that part of Israel that was not deported in the Babylonian exile of 587 B.C. The Gentiles may also be included.

3. The Justification of the Ungodly

Although the precise language of the "justification of the ungodly" does not yet appear, the idea is materially present already in important sections of the Old Testament. Otfried Hofius has shown this in a fine essay.[3] Thus, for example, Abra-

---

[2]Bernd Janowski, "Er trug unsere Sünden: Jes 53 und die Dramatik der Stellvertretung," in *Der leidende Gottesknecht*, ed. B. Janowski and P. Stuhlmacher (Tübingen: Mohr Siebeck, 1996), p. 43 (27-48).
[3]Otfried Hofius, "'Rechtfertigung des Gottlosen' als Thema biblischer Theologie," in *Paulusstudien*, ed. B. Janowski and P. Stuhlmacher (Tübingen: Mohr Siebeck, 1989), pp. 121-47.

ham is chosen apart from all merit according to the Yahwistic tradition of election in Genesis 12:1-3; Israel is shown grace by God out of his free divine love and mercy according to Hosea 11:8-9; and Second Isaiah expresses himself very similarly concerning Yahweh's demonstrations of mercy and salvation to Israel (cf. Is 43:25; 44:21-22; 45:17). Moreover, the Old Testament "grace formula"[4] disproves the widespread idea that the Old Testament speaks above all of God's wrath and vengeance. The formula runs: "[Yahweh is] a merciful and gracious God, slow to anger, and abounding in steadfast love and faithfulness, keeping steadfast love for the thousandth generation, forgiving iniquity and transgression and sin" (Ex 34:6-7). The use of this formula in the Decalogue in Exodus 20:5-6 contrasts it with the language of a God who is jealous against transgressors of his will. To be sure, the one God punishes the iniquity of the fathers down to the great-grandchildren, but his grace reaches much further, to the thousandth generation (cf. also Deut 7:9; Is 54:7-8). The jealous God is therefore put in the shade by the much more gracious God, and his judgments are not an end in themselves but only the means to establish righteousness and welfare over against all injustice.

4. God's Righteousness

The expression "God's righteousness" (δικαιοσύνη θεοῦ) occurs repeatedly in Paul's letters: 2 Corinthians 5:21; Romans 1:17; 3:21, 22, 25, 26; 10:3.[5] In Philippians 3:9 Paul speaks moreover of "the righteousness from God" (ἡ ἐκ θεου δικαιοσύνη). These con-

---

[4]The term "grace-formula" was phrased by Hermann Spieckermann in his essay "Barmherzig und gnädig ist der Herr" (*ZAW* 102 [1990]: 1-18).

[5]Compare Peter Stuhlmacher, *Paul's Letter to the Romans*, trans. S. J. Hafemann (Louisville, Ky.: Westminster John Knox, 1994), pp. 29-32; Mark Seifrid, *Justification by Faith* (Leiden: Brill, 1992), pp. 78-135; and Mark Seifrid, *Christ, Our Righteousness* (Downers Grove, Ill.: InterVarsity Press, 2000), pp. 35-47.

structions go back to the Old Testament and early Judaism. According to Judges 5:11; 1 Samuel 12:7; Psalm 103:6; Daniel 9:16 and Micah 6:56, the history of Israel is filled with "the righteous acts of the LORD" (יהוה צִדְקוֹת). These signify salvation and deliverance for the threatened people of God; hence some English versions translate not merely as *"righteous* acts" but as the *"saving* acts" or the *"saving* justice" of the Lord.[6] These saving acts are also praised in the Rule of the Community at Qumran (cf. 1QS 10:23). In Second Isaiah (cf. Is 45:8, 23-24; 51:6, 8) and in Psalms (71:19; 89:17; 96:13; 98:9; 111:3), God's righteousness is considered the quintessential activity to create salvation and well being. The righteousness of God is also active in judgment, giving security and hope to those without legal rights (cf. Is 1:26-27) and denouncing the wicked (cf. Ps 50:6-7). In the penitential prayers of the Old Testament, God's righteousness is appealed to as his saving mercy. Hence with the texts mentioned above (1QS 11:10-15; 4 Ezra 8:31-36), we may compare especially Daniel 9:16, 18:

> O Lord, in view of all your righteous acts, let your anger and wrath, we pray, turn away from your city Jerusalem. . . . We do not present our supplication before you on the ground of our righteousness, but on the ground of your great mercies. (NRSV)

In sum, *"God's righteousness" in the Old Testament and early Judaism means, above all, the activity of the one God to create welfare and salvation in the creation, in the history of Israel, and in the situation of the (end-time) judgment.*

5. To Justify and to Be Justified

Returning to Paul and Romans, it becomes clear that Paul's discourse about justification is of Old Testament and early Jewish

---

[6]Compare the NRSV and the NJB at 1 Samuel 12:7; Micah 6:5.

origin and has a forensic ring to it. When the verb δικαιοῦν, "to justify," is used in the active voice, it designates God's act of justification (cf. Gal 3:8; Rom 3:26, 30; 4:5; 8:30, 33). The passive δικαιοῦσθαι, "to be justified," usually means in Paul the acceptance that is extended to or withheld from humans in the judgment (cf. Gal 2:16-17; 3:11, 24; Rom 2:13; 3:20, 24, 28). However, the passive δικαιοῦσθαι also occurs once for the acknowledgment that sinners must pay the just God in the final judgment (cf. Rom 3:5 with Ps 51:4). The expression "to reckon as righteousness" (λογίζεσθαι εἰς δικαιοσύνην) describes the acknowledgment of righteous deeds in the final judgment by God (cf. Gal 3:6; Rom 4:3-5 with Gen 15:6), while the noun δικαίωσις in Romans 4:25 and 5:18 stands for the process and result of the justification carried out by God. In typical Jewish manner Paul talks about the righteousness of God "synthetically."[7] He uses it to designate God's own creative and saving activity (e.g., Rom 3:5, 25-26) as well as the grace gift of righteousness in which believers share (e.g., Rom 3:22; 2 Cor 5:21). Ernst Käsemann therefore spoke aptly of "the insoluble compound of power and gift" that determines the Pauline discourse about God's righteousness.[8]

6. The Traditions About Justification Prior to Paul

Paul's statements about justification are not merely reflections of the Old Testament and early Jewish faith tradition.[9] The apos-

---

[7]Compare Karl Hj. Fahlgren, Ṣedaqā nahestehende und entgegengesetzte Begriffe im Alten Testament (Uppsala, Sweden: Almquist & Wiksells, 1932), p. 51: The Israelites' concept of life "ist synthetisch, so daß all das, was für uns etwas Selbständiges ist, ihm nur als verschiedene Seiten derselben Sache erscheint."
[8]Ernst Käsemann, "Gottesgerechtigkeit bei Paulus," in Exegetische Versuche und Besinnungen II (Göttingen: Vandenhoeck & Ruprecht, 1964), p. 187 (181-93).
[9]Compare Peter Stuhlmacher, Reconciliation, Law, and Righteousness, trans. E. R. Kalin (Philadelphia: Fortress, 1986), pp. 50-67.

tle was led to his teachings when the crucified Jesus appeared to him in divine glory on the way to Damascus and called him to be his "minister to the Gentiles" (cf. Rom 15:16 with Gal 1:13-17; 1 Cor 15:9-10). After this spectacular call, Paul was baptized into the Christian community in Damascus (cf. Acts 9:18) and became more exactly acquainted with their doctrinal traditions. However, once Paul himself became active as a missionary, he had to coordinate his own apostolic commission and teaching with the office and doctrinal tradition of the apostles appointed before him.

6.1 Paul reached this agreement by stressing the sacred independence of his missionary commission over against that of the other apostles but also by submitting his gospel to the Jerusalem "pillars" for examination (cf. Gal 2:2). He received their approval, and he emphasizes in 1 Corinthians 15:1-11 that he preaches the same gospel as all the other apostles. In verses 3-5 he even quotes it verbatim:

Christ died for our sins in accordance with the scriptures,
and he was buried,
and he was raised on the third day in accordance with the scriptures,
and he appeared to Cephas, then to the twelve.

In this easily learned four-line faith formula, the death of Jesus is understood from the perspective of Isaiah 53:10-12 as death "for our sins." It was probably Jesus himself who provided the impetus for this interpretation of his death on the cross (cf. Mk 10:45 par. and 14:24 par.). This is especially important for the theology of justification because Isaiah 53:11 says that God's servant will justify many through his sufferings. Christology and justification are connected for the apostles, including Paul, especially on the basis of Isaiah 53:10-12. One can read the same thing in Romans 4:25, where Paul quotes another christological formula: Jesus our Lord "was handed over to death (by God) for our trespasses and was raised (by God) for our justification." *Christological statements about justification were thus already given to Paul in the apostolic faith tradition, which he inherited.*

6.2 Paul quotes and comments upon the boldest of the pre-Pauline traditions about justification in Romans 3:25:

> God installed him (i.e., Christ) publicly as the place of atonement (ἱλαστήριον) by virtue of his blood, as a demonstration of his (i.e., God's) righteousness through the remission of the sins previously committed under God's patience.

In this text, which presumably goes back to the Stephen circle in Jerusalem,[10] Jesus' death and God's righteousness are connected not by means of Isaiah 53:11 but through the christological exposition of Leviticus 16, that is, the Day of Atonement tradition. Good Friday is the eschatological Day of Atonement for the Christian church.[11] Jesus' death on the cross on Golgatha is the great divine sin offering, effective through Jesus' sacrificial blood. God installed Christ as the "place of atonement" (ἱλαστή-ριον; בַּכַּפֹּרֶת) for the demonstration (ἔνδειξις) of his (saving!) righteousness. He demonstrates his righteousness by effecting through the sacrificial death of his Son the remission of all the sins committed during the period of his patience (with Israel). Much as in Romans 2:4, ἀνοχή here means the patience that God exercises toward his own special people, δικαιοσύνη θεοῦ can be interpreted, if one will, as God's covenant faithfulness, which creates for the people of God by free grace the forgiveness of those sins that preceded the appearance of Jesus Christ and faith in him.

[10]Ibid., pp. 94-109.
[11]Compare J. Roloff, *Exegetisches Wörterbuch zum Neuen Testament* (Stuttgart: Kohlhammer, 1981), 2:456.

6.3 We come full circle once we assume (with Christoph Burchard and Michael Theobald) that Paul's fundamental doctrinal statement, built on Psalm 143:2 ("a person is justified not by the works of the law but through faith in Jesus Christ," Gal 2:16; cf. Rom 3:28), may be traced back to the missionary congregation in Antioch and through it perhaps even to the Stephen circle.[12] Paul could fit his own insights into the revelation of Christ and its consequences so effectively into this statement that it became the distinguishing feature of his own doctrine of justification. The saying quoted in 1 Corinthians 6:11 about the baptized being washed (from their sins), sanctified and justified in baptism also seems to have pre-Pauline roots.

6.4 From the aforementioned traditional texts it can be seen that Paul built his doctrine of justification on the basis of the holy Scriptures and the doctrinal traditions that had already been developed before him, both in the early church in Jerusalem and in the missionary churches of Damascus and Antioch. *The Pauline doctrine of justification has ecumenical roots.* It gains its special profile from the fact that Paul incorporated his own experience of God's calling into the justification tradition and then bound together the individual statements about it thematically. He saw himself "accepted" (cf. Rom 15:7) by the grace of the living Christ on the road to Damascus; he understood the gospel of God concerning Jesus Christ that was entrusted to him to be the message of the revelation of God's righteousness; and he gave the "word of reconciliation" (2 Cor 5:19), which God had

---

[12]Compare Christoph Burchard, "Nicht aus Werken des Gesetzes gerecht, sondern aus Glauben an Jesus Christus—seit wann?" in *Geschichte-Tradition-Reflexion: Festschrift für M. Hengel,* ed. H. Lichtenberger (Tübingen: Mohr Siebeck, 1996), 3:405-15; Michael Theobald, "Der Kanon von der Rechtfertigung (Gal 2,16; Röm 3,28)—Eigentum des Paulus oder Gemeingut der Kirche?" in *Worum geht es in der Rechtfertigungslehre?* ed. Th. Söding (Freiburg: Herder, 1999), pp. 131-92.

established as a direct counterpoint to the revelation at Sinai,[13] its proper place within the global horizon of apostolic missionary activity.

7. Paul's Call to Be an Apostle of Jesus Christ

The apostle Paul made his personal stake in justification clear to his beloved congregation in Philippi as they too were threatened by Jewish-Christian false teachings that declared Paul's gospel to be in need of supplementation. Aroused by anger over the appearance of these people, the apostle writes in Philippians 3:4-11:

> If anyone else has reason to be confident in the flesh, I have more: circumcised on the eighth day, a member of the people of Israel, of the tribe of Benjamin, a Hebrew born of Hebrews; as to the law, a Pharisee; as to zeal, a persecutor of the church; as to righteousness under the law, blameless.
>
> Yet whatever gains I had, these I have come to regard as loss because of Christ. More than that, I regard everything as loss because of the surpassing value of knowing Christ Jesus my Lord. For his sake I have suffered the loss of all things, and I regard them as rubbish [or literally "dung," as in the King James Version], in order that I may gain Christ and be found in him, not having a righteousness of my own that comes from the law, but one that comes through faith in Christ, the righteousness from God based on faith. I want to know Christ and the power of his resurrection and the sharing of his sufferings by becoming like him in his death, if somehow I may attain the resurrection from the dead. (NRSV)

Here we have all in one place the elements of the event of justification that Paul considered essential. The young Paul, proud of

---

[13]For this counterpoint compare νόμον ἔθετο ἐν Ἰσραήλ (Ps 77:5 LXX) with θέμενος ἐν ἡμῖν τὸν λόγον τῆς καταλλαγῆς (2 Cor 5:19), and Otfried Hofius, "Gott hat unter uns aufgerichtet das Wort von der Versöhnung (2 Kor 5,19)," in Paulusstudien, ed. B. Janowski and P. Stuhlmacher (Tübingen: Mohr Siebeck, 1989), pp. 15-32.

...s impeccable Jewish heritage and pharisaic way of life, had persecuted the church of God and of his Christ out of zeal for the Torah (cf. Gal 1:13-14). After all, the church with its confession of Christ and its orientation toward Christ's instruction (cf. Gal 6:2) seemed to have broken with the Sinai covenant. But then when he was surprised on his way to Damascus by the appearance of the living Christ, Paul could see—and had to see—that the brilliance of the glory of God on the face of the exalted Christ far exceeded the glory of the Torah (cf. 2 Cor 3:11 with 4:6). At the same time, he had to admit that his holy zeal for the Torah had not brought him closer to God but rather had made him a fighter against God's ways in Christ. *Ever since then, sin for Paul consisted not only of individual transgressions of the commandments but could also include pious zeal for those commandments.* Armed with the knowledge that the crucified and exalted Christ is the Son of God to whom God had given the divine name "Lord" (κύριος) (cf. Phil 2:6-11), Paul gave up everything that had previously been near and dear to him. His righteousness, based on the law, he now considered worthless and mere "dung" (σκύβαλα). Instead the real point for him was the gift of the righteousness by faith that comes from God. His whole thought and endeavor were aimed at knowing Christ Jesus even more deeply, sharing in his sufferings and then attaining the resurrection from the dead through the fellowship of these sufferings, as God has promised to those who are his (cf. Phil 3:20-21). It is hard to imagine a more radical turnaround in life than the one described here.

7.1 This turnaround made Paul the apostle to the Gentiles, but it also brought him lifelong enmity from his former Jewish friends, who could hardly see in the apostle anything other than an apostate. They took action against Paul in the same way he had done against the Christians before him, and they also attempted to hinder his preaching of the gospel (cf. 1 Thess 2:16; 2 Cor 11:24). Added to this was the criticism from Jewish Christians. From the beginning they had mistrusted the radicalness with which Paul had suddenly begun speaking against the law and for Jesus Christ (cf. Acts 9:26). But they did not want to move away from the Torah as far as the apostle himself did, and so after the so-called Antioch incident (cf. Gal 2:11-21), they organized a regular countermission against him that was effective as far as Rome. Paul dealt with his Jewish-Christian opponents harshly and sarcastically (cf. Gal 2:4-5; Rom 3:8; 15:18-21; Phil 3:2), but from the first letter to the Corinthians onward, he also clearly showed that the accusation that he wanted to do away with the law was completely unjustified (cf. 1 Cor 7:19; Rom 6:1, 15; 7:7, 12, 14; 8:4; 9:4).

7.2 Regarding the question of the law, Paul was not able to reach complete agreement with the great apostles before and beside him. Nevertheless, he never broke with Peter, nor with James the Lord's brother. The one gospel of Christ that bound them to him and him to them seems to have been more important for all three of them than the individual questions of soteriology and ethics. What held these men together under this gospel was their parallel experience of Christ's call. The living Christ had "accepted" them again after severe failures (cf. Lk 15:2; Rom 15:7) and had enlisted them in his service. Peter had betrayed Jesus, and he became the bedrock of the church of God and of his Christ (cf. Mt 16:18) only because Jesus interceded for him and appeared to him as the first of his former μαθηταί (cf. Lk 22:32; 24:34; 1 Cor 15:5). James the Lord's brother did not seem to think much of his brother during his lifetime (cf. Mk 3:21; Jn 7:5) and was led to a knowledge of Christ only through the Easter appearance, which was also made to him (cf. 1 Cor 15:7). Peter, James and Paul all had an experience of gracious acceptance (justification) by the risen Christ, and this is what kept them from denouncing each other.

7.3 Paul saw himself as called by the risen Christ to preach the gospel of God concerning Jesus Christ above all to the Gentiles (cf. Gal 1:16; Rom 1:5; 15:16). He was thus involved in a special way in the ministry of mission to the nations that the exalted Christ had given Peter and the other disciples in Galilee (cf. Mt 28:19).[14] Beginning in Jerusalem they carried out this ministry in the conviction that the parousia of Christ would only come once the gospel of the kingdom of God had been proclaimed "throughout whole world, as a testimony to all the nations" (cf. Mt 24:14; Mk 13:10). Paul defined the geographical goals and extent of his missionary commission above all from the holy Scriptures (cf. Gal 1:17; 2 Cor 4:4-6 with Is 49:1, 6; 42:6-7, 11, 16,[15] and Rom 15:16-28 with Is 52:15; 66:18-21).[16] But he also had to coordinate his activities practically with the Jerusalem apostles. This happened above all at the so-called apostolic council in Jerusalem. Here it was formally agreed that the Jerusalem "pillars" would take the gospel to the Jews, while Barnabas and Paul would take it to the Gentiles. They could leave the Gentiles whom they converted uncircumcized, but they had to take up a collection among them for the poor in the original church to show the solidarity of the mission churches with the mother church in Jerusalem materially and practically (cf. Rom 15:25-28 with Gal 2:1-10). Paul kept to this agreement.

---

[14]Compare Peter Stuhlmacher, "Matthew 28:16-20 and the Course of Mission in the Apostolic and Postapostolic Age," in The Mission of the Early Church to Jews and Gentiles, ed. J. Ådna and H. Kvalbein (Tübingen: Mohr Siebeck, 2000), pp. 17-43.

[15]Compare Seyoon Kim, The Origin of Paul's Gospel, 2nd ed. (Tübingen: Mohr Siebeck, 1984), pp. 60, 91-96, and his essay "Isaiah 42 and Paul's Call" (forthcoming).

[16]Compare Rainer Riesner, Paul's Early Period (Grand Rapids, Mich.: Eerdmans, 1998), pp. 231-63.

He carried out his mission in the eastern Mediterranean world "from Jerusalem as far around as Illyricum" (Rom 15:19). He understood himself as the special servant of Jesus Christ to the Gentiles, and so he is to "delay" the end-time events long enough for the mission to be completed in the sense of Mark 13:10 and Matthew 24:14 (cf. 2 Thess 2:6-7; Rom 11:25).[17] Finally, in bringing the collection to Jerusalem he lost first his freedom and then his life.

8. William Wrede and Albert Schweitzer

From our brief sketch it will be clear that for Paul the gospel of God concerning Jesus Christ is a power of God that concerns all people and determines the course of salvation history (cf. Rom 1:16-17). This apocalyptic breadth of the doctrine of justification must not be diminished by limiting the gospel of God's righteousness to the message of the forgiveness of sins for individual sinners who confess Jesus as Lord and Savior. What is involved in the demonstration of God's righteousness through the atoning death of Christ and in his resurrection for the justification of many and in his ongoing activity as Lord, Advocate, Savior and Judge of the world is nothing less than the establishment of the right of God over the whole cosmos.[18]

---

[17]Second Thessalonians 2:6-7 causes exegetical problems, but the least problematic solution to them is still Oscar Cullmann's proposal to understand vv. 6-7 in the light of Mk 13:10 (Mt 24:14) and to identify Paul himself with the κατέχων; compare Cullmann's essay "Der eschatologische Charakter des Missionsauftrags und des apostolischen Selbstbewußtseins bei Paulus," in *Vorträge und Aufsätze 1925-1962*, ed. K. Fröhlich (Tübingen: Mohr Siebeck; Zürich: Zwingli, 1966), pp. 305-36, and P. Stuhlmacher, *Biblische Theologie des Neuen Testaments II* (Göttingen: Vandenhoeck & Ruprecht, 1999), pp. 54-59.

[18]According to Ernst Käsemann, δικαιοσύνη θεοῦ is for the apostle Paul "jenes Recht, mit welchem sich Gott in der von ihm gefallenen und als Schöpfung doch unverbrüchlich ihm gehörenden Welt durchsetzt" ("Gottesgerechtigkeit bei Paulus," p. 92).

In 1904 William Wrede proposed the thesis that the doctrine of justification is not Paul's primary doctrine but only his "polemical doctrine." It becomes "understandable from [Paul's] life struggles, his disputes with Judaism and Jewish Christianity," and it was supposedly developed only for these disputes.[19] But this thesis leads just as surely into error as does its revival by Albert Schweitzer. In 1930 Schweitzer wrote, "The doctrine of righteousness by faith is a subsidiary crater, which has formed within the rim of the main crater, the mystical doctrine of redemption through the being-in-Christ."[20] It is clear from Galatians and Philippians that the Jewish and Jewish-Christian opponents of the apostle did in fact play a role in the formation of Paul's doctrine of justification. But this doctrine is not exhausted by its polemical use against the so-called Judaizers. This is shown by Paul's report of his call in Philippians 3:4-11 as well as by the relatively unpolemical statements about justification in 1 Corinthians 1:30; 6:11; 2 Corinthians 5:21. The polemical accents also fade into the background in the comprehensive presentation of his gospel in Romans.

For the apostle Paul, the gospel of God's righteousness involves precisely that which Wrede and Schweitzer disputed, namely the faith-producing message of salvation for Jews and Gentiles par excellence. Paul understood by justification not only the forgiveness of sins but rather first and foremost the end-time forensic work of salvation that God, through his crucified and exalted Christ, carries out on behalf of all humanity. If one thinks through the texts about the vicarious atoning death of Jesus in 2 Corinthians 5:21 and Romans 3:25-26 in Jewish-Christian categories, then a dichotomy in Paul between a juristic

---

[19]William Wrede, *Paulus,* 2nd ed. (Tübingen: Mohr Siebeck, 1907), p. 72.
[20]Albert Schweitzer, *Die Mystik des Apostels Paulus* (Tübingen: Mohr Siebeck, 1930), p. 220.

doctrine of redemption oriented around justification and a mystical or participatory doctrine of redemption oriented around being in Christ is out of the question. Believers in Jesus Christ already participate in Jesus' death and new life through their baptism, but they remain filled with the hope of righteousness (cf. Gal 5:5) because they walk not by sight, but at first only by faith. According to Paul, Israel was elected for justification through Jesus the Christ already in Abraham. But this election has not yet been fulfilled. It will come to fulfillment only when "all Israel" has been redeemed from its sins and brought to the goal of its election by the Christ-Deliverer who will come from Zion (cf. Rom 11:26). Justification for the apostle is the quintessential structural law of God's gracious work in salvation history: "God has imprisoned all (Gentiles and Jews) in disobedience so that he may be merciful to all (in and through Christ)" (Rom 11:32).

9. Conclusions

Looking back, we have gained a whole series of important exegetical insights. We have recalled the Old Testament Jewish background, the early Christian ecumenical roots and the forensic horizon of the Pauline doctrine of justification. We have seen that the gospel of God's righteousness that Paul proclaimed is not exhausted by the message of the forgiveness of sins for individual Jews and Gentiles. Rather, it involves the saving message, which must be passed on to all the peoples of the world, concerning the end-time rule of God that the one God will establish through his Christ. The spreading of this message by the Jerusalem apostles and Paul moves history toward its goal, and "justification" designates the quintessence of the creative, gracious dealings of God with Gentiles and Jews. The crucified and risen Christ is for the apostle the messianic Lord of the world appointed by God. As such, he has a threefold task. He is God's guarantor of the justification of all those who confess him as Lord and Savior, from the day of his exaltation to the right hand of God until the final judgment (cf. 1 Cor 1:30; Rom 8:34). He is the judge of the world, appointed by God himself (cf. 2 Cor 5:10; Rom 2:16). And he has the mission of delivering "all Israel" (cf. Rom 11:26). The goal of his activity is the establishment of God's kingdom and reign (cf. 1 Cor 15:23-28).

TWO

GOD'S RIGHTEOUSNESS & GOD'S KINGDOM

W hat I have said up until now concerning the theme of justification is consistent with the traditional evaluation of the message of justification by many of today's Protestant and Catholic interpreters of Paul. But this agreement conceals a problem that must be addressed. Since 1963 massive objections against the traditional view of the Pauline doctrine of justification have been raised (mainly) by Krister Stendahl, E. P. Sanders and James D. G. Dunn. We must therefore ask whether we can really understand Paul along the lines followed up until now; we cannot rest content simply to reaffirm that particular theological interpretation of Paul that, in the English-speaking world, is readily abbreviated and critically (or rather uncritically) designated as "Lutheran." The issue behind the criticism has recently been put in a nutshell by Karl-Wilhelm Niebuhr in his essay "The Pauline Doctrine of Justification in Current Exegetical Dis-

cussion."[1] Niebuhr says that behind the critical use of the term
Lutheran

> stands the view that those categories and thought patterns of
> Pauline interpretation that have especially characterized German
> Protestant exposition, such as the opposition of grace and merit,
> or righteousness by faith and righteousness by works, have devel-
> oped from Luther's dispute with the medieval practice of pen-
> ance in the Catholic church but do not apply to those positions on
> the Jewish law with which Paul had to interact. The target of such
> inquiries is above all the understanding of Paul by Rudolf Bult-
> mann and his students.[2]

1. The "New Perspective on Paul"

In order to be clear about the occasion and background for the criticism of Stendahl, Sanders and Dunn, we must know two things.
First, we must be aware of Luther's Reformation discovery and its
epoch-making consequences. We must also keep in mind the
apparent goal of these authors to make a new beginning in Pauline
interpretation, so as to free Jewish-Christian dialogue from
improper accusations against the Jewish conversation partners.

1.1 Luther writes about the first point in the preface to the
complete edition of his Latin writings in 1545.[3] There he recalls
that his epochal insight, namely that *iustitia dei* in Romans 1:17
refers not to God's penal justice but rather to the salvation that
God opens up to believers, came to him while he was meditating
on Romans 1:16–17:

> At last, by the mercy of God, meditating day and night, I gave
> heed to the context of the words, namely, "In it the righteousness

---

[1]Karl-Wilhelm Niebuhr, "Die paulinische Rechtfertigungslehre in der gegenwär-
tigen exegetischen Diskussion" in *Worum geht es in der Rechtfertigungslehre?* ed.
Th. Söding (Freiburg: Herder, 1999), pp. 106-10.
[2]Ibid., p. 107.
[3]*WA* 54, no. 185: 14ff.

of God is revealed, as it is written, 'He who through faith is righteous shall live!'" There I began to understand that the righteousness of God is that by which the righteous lives by a gift of God, namely by faith. And this is the meaning: the righteousness of God is revealed by the gospel, namely, the passive righteousness with which merciful God justifies us by faith, as it is written, "He who through faith is righteous shall live." Here I felt that I was altogether born again and had entered paradise itself through open gates. There a totally other face of the entire Scripture showed itself to me. Thereupon I ran though the Scriptures from memory. I also found in other terms an analogy, as, the word of God, that is, what God does in us, the power of God, with which he makes us strong, the wisdom of God, with which he makes us wise, the strength of God, the salvation of God, the glory of God. And I extolled my sweetest word with a love as great as the hatred with which I had before hated the word "righteousness of God." Thus that place in Paul was for me truly the gate to paradise.[4]

This exegetical discovery made Luther a reformer. It led him to see Paul's teaching about the justification of the sinner by faith alone as the definitive center of the entire biblical message of salvation. But the further Luther came into conflict with the representatives of the traditional Catholic doctrine of justification for the sake of his new view of justification, the more he identified himself with Paul's struggle against Judaizing false teachers and Jewish opponents. Luther saw the Jewish and Jewish-Christian adversaries of Paul as one with the Catholic theologians of his time, while he and his followers appeared in the role of Paul and his pupils. This blurring of the distinction between historical and dogmatic perspectives remains a factor in German Pauline scholarship to this day.

1.2 Nevertheless, as early as 1929 Werner Georg Kümmel, in

---

[4]Martin Luther, *Works* 34:337.

his famous dissertation on *Romans 7 and the Conversion of Paul,*[5] worked out the distinction between Paul's conversion and Luther's Reformation discovery. In 1938 Paul Althaus (under the influence of Adolf Schlatter) pointed out the differences between the Pauline and the Lutheran doctrines of justification.[6] After the Second World War, Wilfried Joest underscored this differences in important works.[7] But these distinctions did not hinder Kümmel, Althaus and Joest any more than they stopped Rudolf Bultmann and his students from continuing to consider Luther's soteriological intensification and theological evaluation of Paul's doctrine of justification to be correct and trailblazing. They accepted that because of this evaluation of Paul's doctrine, the Catholic understanding of justification remained saddled with the verdict of "works-righteousness." Nor they did not shy away from placing the Jewish-Christians and Jews who opposed the historical Paul under the same verdict. In view of the characterization of the soteriology of ancient Judaism by Paul Billerbeck in his famous *Commentary on the New Testament from the Talmud and Midrash,*[8] there was no historical reason for these authors to distance themselves from this judgment.

1.3 However, the texts discovered in Qumran did provide a reason for correcting the picture of ancient Judaism that had held sway until the middle of the twentieth century. To the extent that these corrections were made, the interpretation of Paul indebted to the Reformation with its characterization of the

---

[5]Werner Georg Kümmel, *Römer 7 und die Bekehrung des Paulus,* reprinted in W. G. Kümmel, *Römer 7 und das Bild des Menschen im Neuen Testament* (München: Kaiser, 1974).

[6]Paul Althaus, *Paulus und Luther über den Menschen,* 2nd ed. (1938; reprint, Gütersloh: Bertelsmann, 1951).

[7]Compare above all W. Joest, *Gesetz und Freiheit* 3rd ed. (Göttingen: Vandenhoeck & Ruprecht, 1961).

[8]Paul Billerbeck, *Kommentar zum Neuen Testament aus Talmud und Midrasch,* vol. IV/1 (München: Beck, 1928), pp. 3-6.

apostle's Jewish opponents as champions of works-righteousness gave offense and called forth a counterreaction. Since 1961
Krister Stendahl in several lectures and essays has stressed
again the already well-known difference between the converted
Pharisee Paul and the Augustinian monk Martin Luther, driven
by pangs of conscience. Stendahl, appealing to Albert Schweitzer
(see chapter one), also held that the doctrine of justification did
not represent the center of Paul's message of salvation. By
insisting that justification was available not through the works of
the law but only through faith in Jesus Christ, the apostle to the
Gentiles supposedly wanted only to ensure pragmatically that
the Gentiles entrusted to him could share in the same privileges
of salvation as Israel (cf. Eph 2:11-22). Stendahl's essays appeared in 1976 in a slender volume titled *Paul Among Jews and
Gentiles*.[9] Ernst Käsemann sharply contradicted this devaluation
of justification by Stendahl and proposed instead the thesis that
"God's Basileia is the content of the Pauline doctrine of justification."[10] But exegetical research has had a hard time coming to
terms with this correct counterthesis. It fitted as little into the
dialogue that Stendahl wanted to have with Jews as it did into
the fixed framework of Bultmann's program to demythologize
and interpret the Pauline texts existentially.

    1.4 When E. P. Sanders published his famous work *Paul and
Palestinian Judaism* in 1977,[11] ancient Judaism appeared once for
all in a new light in the English-speaking world. Sanders freed
Palestinian Judaism from its negative reputation of works-righteousness and of illegitimate self-praise (boasting) before God by

---

[9]Krister Stendahl, *Paul Among Jews and Gentiles* (Philadelphia: Fortress, 1976).
[10]Ernst Käsemann, "Rechtfertigung und Heilsgeschichte im Römerbrief," in *Paulinische Perspektiven* (Tübingen: Mohr Siebeck, 1969), p. 133 (108-39).
[11]E. P. Sanders, *Paul and Palestinian Judaism* (London: SCM Press; Philadelphia:
Fortress, 1977).

bringing out afresh the meaning of the covenant. According to Sanders, the Sinai covenant is the great gift of God's grace to his chosen people Israel. Access to this covenant cannot and need not be earned by Israel but is rather opened to Israel by divine grace. Once the Israelites are accepted into the covenant, they only have to stay within it and prove themselves to be members of the covenant people. When they fall into sin, they must repent and offer sacrifices. But here they may trust in divine forgiveness because repentance and the sacrificial cult are already provided for in the covenant. Therefore, for Sanders, "covenantal nomism" constitutes the center of ancient Jewish religion. Instead of accusing Judaism of works-righteousness, one can and must see it as a religion of grace. Unfortunately, Sanders's brief book on Paul in 1991[12] shows that he expended much less effort on the interpretation of Paul than he did on the analysis of the rabbinic sources. Sanders's appraisal of the status of justification in Paul's thought is very similarly to Stendahl's. In asserting that Paul considered participation in Christ and being in Christ to be much more important than justification, Sanders has recourse once again to Albert Schweitzer's distinction between a peripheral justification and a central Christ mysticism in Paul.

1.5 Along slightly different lines James D. G. Dunn was and still is deeply impressed by Sanders's presentation of ancient Judaism, but he considers Sanders's picture of Paul to be inadequate. Since his encounter with Sanders, Dunn has invested a truly enormous amount of effort into giving Pauline interpretation a new direction. He does this by placing not only ancient Judaism but also the apostle's own theology under the rubric of "covenantal nomism." In a programmatic lecture delivered in 1983, Dunn developed what he called the "New Perspective on

---

[12]E. P. Sanders, *Paul* (Oxford: Oxford University Press, 1991).

Paul."[13] Not only did Dunn proceed to make this new perspective the foundation of his two-volume commentary on Romans,[14] he also presupposed it in his exegesis of Galatians,[15] developed it in many essays, and finally summarized it again in his important textbook *The Theology of Paul the Apostle.*[16] How readily the new perspective has been adopted can be seen for example in the popular presentation by N. T. Wright in his book *What Saint Paul Really Said.*[17] Drawing upon Sanders and Stendahl, Dunn holds above all to two basic insights: (1) Ancient Judaism is not a religion of works-righteousness and boasting before God but a religion of the prevenient grace of God. It knows justification by faith and lives in it. The only danger for Judaism is that it might seek to keep the covenant to itself and to exclude the Gentiles from it by making circumcision, food laws and sabbath observance into conditions for covenant membership. Dunn is convinced that whoever does not share his view is endangered by implicit or explicit antisemitism. (2) The apostle's teaching of justification apart from the works of the law is first and foremost about the soteriological equality of Jews and Gentiles before God. Paul wants to present both groups, Jews and Gentiles, to the one God who in Christ is graciously inclined toward them, accepts them both and obligates them equally to serve him by "faith working through love" (cf. Gal 5:6).

---

[13]James D. G. Dunn, "The New Perspective on Paul," *BJRL* 65 (1983): 95-122; reprinted and expanded in James D. G. Dunn, *Jesus, Paul, and the Law* (London: SPCK, 1990), pp. 183-214.

[14]James D. G. Dunn, *Word Biblical Commentary: Romans 1–8,* and *Word Biblical Commentary: Romans 9–16* (Waco, Tex.: Word, 1988).

[15]James D. G. Dunn, *The Theology of Paul's Letter to the Galatians* (Cambridge: Cambridge University Press, 1993), pp. 75ff., 140ff.

[16]James D. G. Dunn, *The Theology of Paul the Apostle* (Grand Rapids, Mich.: Eerdmans, 1998), pp. 334-89.

[17]N. T. Wright, *What Saint Paul Really Said* (Grand Rapids, Mich.: Eerdmans, 1997).

2. The Deficiencies of the New Perspective

The change in scholarly evaluations of ancient Judaism that E. P. Sanders brought about was an idea whose time had come. Unfortunately, this new picture of ancient Judaism was worked out at the expense not only of Luther's understanding of justification but also of the Pauline doctrine of God's righteousness and justification. Both are regrettable and should be corrected. The deficiencies of the new perspective must therefore now be mentioned, and we concentrate in our context on the exegetical ones.[18]

2.1 As one can readily read in the profound work of Friedrich Avemarie, *Torah and Life,*[19] and in his related essay "Election and Retribution,"[20] *Sanders has given a one-sided picture of the soteriology of ancient Judaism.* Against Billerbeck's thesis of Jewish works-righteousness, Sanders presents his thesis of a religion of grace. But as early as 1939 the Swede Erik Sjöberg[21] had already drawn attention to a fact that Friedrich Avemarie has now worked out in more detail. There are important rabbinic texts about the final judgment that do not allow us to speak simplistically about the principle of grace but rather require two optional views in rabbinic soteriology to be set side by side. In their delib-

---

[18]Important criticism of the "New Perspective" was already delivered by Mark A. Seifrid, *Justification by Faith* (Leiden: Brill, 1992), pp. 46-77; "The 'New Perspective on Paul' and Its Problems," *Themelios* 25, no. 2 (2000): 4-18; and Donald A. Hagner, "Paul and Judaism," *BBR* 3 (1993): 111-30. A renewed version of this substantial essay is enclosed in this volume.

[19]Friedrich Avemarie, *Tora und Leben* (Tübingen: Mohr Siebeck, 1996). In his criticism of the New Perspective, Mark A. Seifrid points to Avemarie's description ("'New Perspective on Paul' and Its Problems," p. 5).

[20]Friedrich Avemarie, "Erwählung und Vergeltung," *NTS* 45 (1999): 108-26. It is noteworthy that Avemarie does not intend an overall criticism of Sanders but only to correct the soteriological one-sidedness in his description of covenantal nomism; compare the appraisal of Sanders's research in Avemarie's essay "Bund als Gabe und Recht," in *Bund und Tora,* ed. F. Avemarie and H. Lichtenberger (Tübingen: Mohr Siebeck, 1996), pp. 163-216.

[21]Erik Sjöberg, *Gott und die Sünder im palästinischen Judentum* (Stuttgart: Kohlhammer, 1939).

erations about the final judgment the rabbis proceed from both a principle of election and a principle of retribution. Their soteriology "is based on two contrary principles, between which there is no fixed relationship, so that they can constantly be brought to bear in different proportions, either with, against, or apart from one another."[22] Rabbinic judgments about grace or retribution in the final judgment therefore often remain in the balance. We have already seen that the same holds true for 4 Ezra (2 Esdras), and we may now add not only 2 Baruch 14:12-13; 51:7-14 but similar evidence from the texts of Qumran: In 1QS we find juxtaposed the claim for perfect and blameless obedience to the law (cf. 3:9-11; 4:2-8; 8:1-10; 9:3-5) and the above (partly) cited penitental doxology in 11:2-15; in 1QpHab 8:1-2 the famous verse Habakkuk 2:4 is related to the observance of the law and faithfulness to the (teachings of the) teacher of righteousness; in 4Q398 (4QMMT^e) frg. 14, col. II:2-7 is clearly testified that obedience to (priestly) works of the law will be reckoned as righteousness to the obedient in the end times.[23] In view of the openness of all these pre- and post-Christian Jewish texts, it is not enough simply to call Judaism a religion of grace and to point to covenantal nomism. There are also serious comments about the end-time significance of (a treasure of) good works, which the faithful should store up during their lives. According to Romans 9:4 Paul thoroughly knew and respected the gift of the Torah to Israel and the covenants that bore up the people of God. But above and beyond these he asked for a precise answer to the question, on what grounds Gentiles and Jews would be saved in

---

[22]Avemarie, "Erwählung," p. 126.

[23]For the concept of justification in Qumran compare Otto Betz, "Rechtfertigung in Qumran," in *Jesus—der Messias Israels* (Tübingen: Mohr Siebeck, 1987), pp. 39-58; and "Göttliche und menschliche Gerechtigkeit in der Gemeinde von Qumran und ihre Bedeutung für das Neue Testament," in *Jesus—Der Herr der Kirche* (Tübingen: Mohr Siebeck, 1990), pp. 275-92.

the final judgment. He failed to find a clear answer to this question in his own Pharisaic tradition, and we can still see historically (e.g., from the Psalms of Solomon) that he had good reason. The answer came to him in his encounter with Jesus Christ. What leads to final salvation is not the keeping of the precepts of the law but only faith in Jesus Christ.

2.2 It is strange that Stendahl and Dunn *evade the question about justification in the final judgment* and thereby obscure the main problem that exercises Paul in Romans. The apostle begins his argument in 1:18–3:20 with a relentless analysis of the culpability of Gentiles and Jews in the judgment. In the final judgment, which has already been announced and which will soon burst upon the scene, no Jew or Gentile will be able to claim that he or she has been a righteous doer of the will of God. Instead all will stand convicted as transgressors of the law. There is hope and justification for Gentiles and Jews only when they confess Jesus to be the Christ whom God has installed on Golgotha as the new "place of atonement" or "mercy seat" (ἱλαστήριον = כַּפֹּרֶת). Whoever believes in this Christ is justified by God (Rom 3:26); whoever does not believe has no prospect of acquittal in the final judgment. The Pauline doctrine of justification is distorted to the extent that this end-time perspective is faded out.

2.3 *The treatment of Galatians 2:16; Romans 3:20, 28* by the main representatives of the new perspective is also strange. They claim that in all three passages Paul merely wanted to correct the Jewish idea that justification can only be received by the members of the covenant people who distinguish themselves from the Gentiles by circumcision, keeping the food laws and purity regulations, and sabbath observance. Paul, on the other hand, wanted to make justification accessible to the Gentiles as well, who made no effort to perform such "works prescribed by the law" (ἔργα νόμου). However, the tradition, history, context and word usage in Galatians 2:16 and Romans 3:20, 28 all fail to support this exposition. As the context shows clearly, Paul formulates three summarizing catechetical statements (בְּכָל־יָם; κεφάλεια) based on Psalm 143:2 (142:2 LXX) and concludes: "No flesh" (σάρξ) or "no person" (ἄνθρωπος) will be justified (by God) on the basis of the "works of the law." Romans 3:9-20 and the future tense in Romans 3:30—God "will justify (δικαιώσει) the circumcised on the ground of faith and the uncircumcised through that same faith"—show that the issue is whether Jews and Gentiles will or will not survive before God's throne of judgment. Before this throne every person will stand laden with guilt and will have to face his or her judgment, namely, destruction. Sin, which holds all people under its sway according to Paul, permits no human life to be in perfect compliance with God's will according to all the commandments of the Torah (cf. Gal 3:10; 5:2). Accordingly, all attempts of humans in the final judgment to build upon their own righteousness derived from the law are futile (cf. Phil 3:9; Rom 10:3). Deliverance comes for all of them only through faith in Jesus Christ.

2.4 Paul was not the first person to speak of the *works of the law*. This expression was already current in ancient Judaism prior to Paul, and it continued after his time. In 4Q398 (= 4QMMTᵉ) frg. 14, col. II,3 the keeping of special cultic regulations is designated as "works of the Torah"; other Qumran texts speak only of "works in the Torah" (cf. 1QS 5:21; 6:18) or simply of "works" (cf. 1QS 5:23, 24) performed in accordance with the Torah (cf. CD 20:6-7). The expression "works" here means the behavior of the members of the community in conformity with the law. The usage of ἔργα and ἔργα νόμου among the Essenes of Qumran is similar to the usage in Paul's letters, and it shows

that Dunn's attempt to distinguish as strictly as possible between "works of the law," involving the so-called Israelite
"boundary markers," and "works" that are ethically relevant, is
artificial. The apostle did not consider the "works of the law" to
be exhausted by keeping the "boundary markers." He himself
equates "works" with obeying God's commandments (cf. Gal 5:6
with 1 Cor 7:19; 2 Cor 9:8; Eph 2:10). Furthermore, the expression "works of the commandments" in 2 Baruch 57:2 refers to
keeping the Torah in general also.

2.5 Finally, to what has already been said we may add that
the new perspective *fails to allow for any clear relationship between christology and justification*. It only reaffirms the erroneous
distinction of justification and Christ mysticism and does not
see that this distinction is due to a deficient understanding of
the atonement. The shortcomings of this new style of interpretation can therefore no longer be overlooked. It wants to present
an alternative to "Lutheran" interpretation, and it has helped us
to consider more carefully the problem of (hidden) anti-Judaism
in Pauline exegesis. Yet it has also truncated Paul's statements
on justification at every step and turn. Things cannot stay that
way.

3. The True Perspective on Paul

Is there then any perspective that will avoid simply placing us
once again on the same beaten track of the theological interpretation of Paul criticized by Stendahl, Sanders and Dunn, while at
the same time making good the deficiencies of the new perspective? Such a perspective does in fact open up if we develop
Stendahl's and Dunn's hints to Paul's self-understanding as the
chosen missionary to the Gentiles and recognize that the apostle
in Romans speaks no less than three times of his apostolic commission to the Gentiles (cf. 1:5-6; 11:13-14; 15:15-24). So all the

statements about justification that we find in Romans stand in the context of Paul's missionary service to the Gentiles. When he wrote this letter, he had only brought his service halfway to completion (cf. 15:22-24).

3.1 When Paul in Romans 4:17 speaks of the one God "who gives life to the dead and calls into existence the things that do not exist," or when he appeals in Romans 15:8-13 to the "God of hope," who in Jesus' mission fulfills the promises given to the patriarchs and who has raised him to life as the messianic ruler in whom the Gentiles shall hope, then he speaks as a Jew converted to faith in Jesus Christ. For the Pharisees the praise of the one God who makes the dead alive was one of the daily requirements of faith, and the discourse about the "God of hope" and his promises arises from the larger context of the Hebrew Bible. The one God whom Israel confesses in the Shema (Deut 6:4) is addressed in Jeremiah 14:8 and 17:13 as the "Hope of Israel" (cf. Jer 50:7). By his promises God had marked out his own special people in the presence of all other peoples. He had performed unparalleled deeds of salvation in Israel's history (cf. Judg 5:11; 1 Sam 12:7; Is 45:24; Mic 6:5; Ps 103:6; Dan 9:16), and he would also effect final salvation and deliverance for Israel (cf., e.g., Is 46:12-13; 51:6; 54:14). Since the time of Second Isaiah, the end-time hopes of Israel were concentrated upon the expectation that God would soon do a new thing (cf. Is 43:19; 51:6; 65:17) and enter his kingly reign upon Mount Zion (cf. Is 40:1-5; 52:7). On that day all God's enemies will be put on trial (Joel 3:9-17; Zech 14), Jerusalem will become the glorious city of God, the Israelites scattered among the peoples will return, and the people of God will be vindicated over against its oppressors (Ezek 36:16-36; Is 62:1-12) and will awake to new life (Ezek 37). In Daniel 2, 7 and 9 the implementation and character of the end-time kingdom of God in Zion are considered more closely. In

Daniel 12:1-3 the resurrection of the dead to glory and to judgment is announced, and in 1 Enoch 61-62 the table fellowship of the righteous with the messianic Son of Man is presented. There was no real dawning of God's kingdom in Zion in the New Testament period, but through the constant praying in the temple of psalms praising God's kingship and kingdom (cf. Ps 93; 96—99) and through the annual liturgy of the popular Feast of Tabernacles, the expectation of the "Zion-βασιλεία" (Hartmut Gese) was kept alive in Israel. In Psalm 81, 84 and 87 it is celebrated proleptically, and in the synagogal Kaddish, as well as in the Eighteen Benedictions, its arrival "soon and swiftly" is prayed for. As a child of tradition-conscious parents (cf. Phil 3:5) who was brought up in Jerusalem and educated as a scribe at the feet of Rabbi Gamaliel I (cf. Acts 22:3), Paul was perfectly familiar with the expectation of God's kingdom in Zion. He celebrated the Feast of Tabernacles as required (cf. Ex 23:14-17; Jubilees 16:20-31), and he certainly prayed the Eighteen Benedictions and the Kaddish.[24] Future expectation for Paul the Jew meant the expectation of the kingdom of God and of his anointed in Zion.

3.2 After his call to be an apostle of Jesus Christ, Paul learned to see the hope of the Zion-βασιλεία in a new way in the light of his personal encounter with the living Christ Jesus. In the risen Jesus who appeared to him on the road to Damascus, Paul recognized the promised messianic Son of God (cf. Gal 1:16; 2 Cor 4:6; 5:16). At the same time, Paul saw himself as chosen to preach the gospel of Christ's kingdom to the Gentiles (Rom 1:1-4; Gal 1:15-16). Paul's being chosen to preach God's gospel about Christ's mission and kingdom put him on the same side as the other apostles called before him to the same service. At the top

---

[24]Compare Martin Hengel, *The Pre-Christian Paul* (London: SCM Press; Philadelphia: Trinity Press, 1991), pp. 34-37.

stood Peter, since he was the first to see the risen Christ (Lk 24:34; 1 Cor 15:5). Because of his position Peter led the disciples of Jesus from Jerusalem to the mountain in Galilee where the risen Christ appeared to them in the universal authority of the Son of Man (cf. Mt 28:16 with Dan 7:14), and then after they received the Great Commission, he led them back to Zion.[25] In Jerusalem, the center of the world as far as salvation history is concerned, Peter founded the circle of the Twelve anew, and the Twelve, together with Mary and the brothers of Jesus, formed the core of the early church (cf. Acts 1:12-26). This group understood itself as the vanguard of the end-time people of God, which Jesus himself had begun to gather. The apostles' task was to gather this people of God fully on behalf of the risen Christ.

At the first Feast of Weeks (Pentecost) after Jesus' crucifixion and resurrection, Peter and the rest of the Twelve began with the preaching of the gospel among the Jewish festival pilgrims (cf. Acts 2:14-41). Then Philip brought the Samaritans within the scope of the Christ mission (cf. Acts 8:4-40), Peter dared to take the next step of baptizing Gentiles in Caesarea (cf. Acts 10:23-48), and Antioch on the Orontes became the center of the Gentile mission. From this city Barnabas and Paul programmatically pursued their mission to the Gentiles (cf. Acts 11:19-26). After it came to a heated debate in Antioch resulting from the first missionary journey of Paul and Barnabas over the question of whether or not the Gentiles converted to faith in Christ still had to be circumcised, the pillar apostles convened the so-called apostolic council in Jerusalem in the year A.D. 48. This council reached a well-known agreement: Peter, James and John would take the gospel to the

---

[25]I have dealt with the course of early Christian mission to Jews and Gentiles in more detail in my essay "Matthew 28:16-20 and the Course of Mission in the Apostolic and Postapostolic Age," in *The Mission of the Early Church to Jews and Gentiles*, ed. J. Ådna and H. Kualbein (Tübingen: Mohr Siebeck, 2000), pp. 17-43.

Jews, while Barnabas and Paul would take it to the Gentiles. The Gentiles did not have to be circumcised. But in the Gentile Christian churches a collection for the poor in the original church was to be taken up as a way of expressing the Gentile Christians' ties with the mother church in Jerusalem (cf. Gal 2:10; Rom 15:26).

From the Gospels, Acts and the Pauline letters the end-time expectations with which the apostles pursued their mission to Jews and Gentiles are still clearly visible. The founding and growth of the early church are equated with the rebuilding of "David's fallen tent" (cf. Acts 15:16 with Amos 9:11-12) and by the witness of the gospel to "all nations" beginning in Jerusalem, the way is to be prepared for the kingdom of God and of his Christ. The keyword "all nations" that defines the Great Commission in Matthew 28:18-20 surfaces in the relevant missions texts again and again (cf. Mk 13:10/Mt 24:14; Lk 24:47; Acts 15:17; Gal 3:8; Rom 1:5; 15:11; 16:26; 2 Tim 4:17). Other formulations supplement this global perspective: preaching of the gospel "in the whole world as a testimony to all nations" (Mt 24:14; cf. also Mk 16:15), apostolic witness "in Jerusalem, in all Judea and Samaria, and to the ends of the earth" (Acts 1:8), etc. The goal of the mission was to orient all nations toward Zion because this is the "mother" of them all (cf. Ps 87:4-6). When this goal has been reached, it is time for the παρουσία of Christ (cf. Mt 28:18-20 with Mt 24:14; Mk 13:10). With it begins the final establishment of the end-time "kingdom for Israel" (βασιλεία τῷ Ἰσραήλ) that Jesus ascribed to his disciples already during his earthly ministry (cf. Lk 12:32 with Dan 7:18) and promised again after his exaltation (cf. Acts 1:6; 3:20-21). This promise of Jesus takes up the early Jewish expectation of the Zion-kingdom of God and of his Anointed and gives it a Christian stamp. Through the Jerusalem apostles Paul had this tradition available to him not only in Jewish but also in Christian form.

3.3 The apostle preached the same gospel as the Jerusalem apostles (cf. 1 Cor 15:1-11) and kept the agreement made at the apostolic council to the last detail. He pursued his mission among the Gentiles "from Jerusalem and as far around as Illyricum" (cf. Rom 15:19) and personally brought the agreed-upon collection to Jerusalem before his planned departure for mission in the west. He also shared the apostolic hope for the end-time establishment of "the kingdom (of God) for Israel" (Acts 1:6). For him Jesus Christ was the "Son of God in power" (Rom 1:4; cf. Phil 2:9), whose task from Psalm 8:6 (Psalm 8:7 Heb.) and 110:1 was to establish the βασιλεία of God. In 1 Corinthians 15:23-28 Paul speaks of the different "stages" or τάγματα for the establishment of the kingdom (cf. NRSV: "each in his own order," 1 Cor 15:23). Moreover, when one takes the Pauline letters as a whole into account and draws on Revelation 19–22 for comparison, one can even attempt to develop a more precise picture of these "stages."[26] The first τάγμα begins with the resurrection and exaltation of Jesus Christ to the right hand of God. The exalted Christ entrusts the apostles with the mission to all nations on earth (cf. Mt 28:16-20 with Rom 10:14-17) and chooses Paul to be his special "servant . . . to the Gentiles" (cf. Gal 1:16; Rom 1:5; 11:13; 15:15-24 with Acts 26:15-18). Through the apostolic world mission the new people of God of Jews and Gentiles is gathered. When this gathering is completed, then *the second* τάγμα begins with the parousia of Christ. It will bring with it the resurrection and transformation of Christians (cf. 1 Thess 4:15-17; 1 Cor 15:51; Phil 3:20-21) and their participation in Christ's kingdom (cf. 1 Cor 6:2-3; Rom 5:17). But the Zion-

---

[26]Compare my essay "Eschatology and Hope in Paul," *EvQ* 72 (2000): 315-33. The schema of Pauline eschatology from there is attached to this lecture also. It illustrates the apocalyptic expectations of the apostle but should *not* be misunderstood as an exact timetable.

βασιλεία will first be established when *the end* (τὸ τέλος) has come. Then the world judgment entrusted to Christ Jesus by God will take place and final justification will occur (cf. Rom 2:5, 16; 14:7-12; 1 Cor 11:32; 2 Cor 5:10; Col 3:6; Eph 5:6), the saints together with Christ will judge the cosmos and the fallen angels (cf. 1 Cor 6:2-3), "all Israel" will be saved through the Christ-Deliverer who comes from Zion (cf. Rom 11:26 with Ps 50:2), Satan and death will be destroyed (cf. Rom 16:20; 1 Cor 15:26), and the creation will be freed from the curse of futility hanging over it since Adam's fall (cf. Rom 8:19-21). Finally, when all beings above the earth, on the earth and under the earth confess that Jesus Christ is Lord, to the glory of God the Father (cf. Phil 2:10-11 with Rom 14:11; Is 49:18), the universe will be reconciled to God and at peace with God through Christ (cf. Col 1:20). Then the Son will hand over the kingdom to the Father (1 Cor 15:24), so that God may once again be all in all (1 Cor 15:28). The center point of this βασιλεία will be Zion according to Romans 11:26-27.

3.4 In view of these statements by the apostle, the virulently contested question of whether Paul thought and taught apocalyptically can only be answered with a clear yes. The imminent establishment of the Zion-βασιλεία was already the main theme of Jewish apocalyptic and of the preaching of the earthly Jesus. In his resurrection early Christianity saw the promising beginning of the end-time resurrection of all the dead (cf. 1 Cor 15:20-22; Rom 1:4; Col 1:18; Rev 1:5), and the church of Jesus Christ was the vanguard of the end-time people of God composed of Jews and Gentiles (cf. Gal 3:26-28; Col 3:9-11; Eph 2:11-18). Paul met the exalted Christ himself and recognized him in the heavens by the royal work entrusted to him by God; he awaited the "day (of the return) of the Lord" in the near future (cf. 1 Thess 4:15; 1 Cor 7:29-31; 15:21-52; Rom 11:30-31; 13:11; 16:20; Phil 4:4-

5). Insofar as 2 Thessalonians goes back to the apostle himself, Paul even understood himself as the chosen messenger of the gospel who would "restrain" the events of the end long enough for the gospel to be preached to all the Gentiles (cf. 2 Thess 2:6-7 with Mk 13:10). In his role as the κατέχων,[27] Paul had to bear the "sufferings of Christ" (2 Cor 1:5) in the service of his Lord, but he could also work toward the coming deliverance of the major-ity of Israel that would remain hardened until the completion of the mission to the nations (cf. Rom 11:13-16). Paul's engagement on behalf of the mother church in Jerusalem (cf. Rom 15:25-33 with Acts 21:15-26) makes perfectly clear that he wanted to be *the apostle to the Gentiles for Israel's sake.* He pursued his mission-ary work in the expectation that the Zion kingdom of God and of his Christ would take on a concrete form in the near future.

3.5 It is within this framework of missionary end-time expec-tation (briefly outlined above) that Paul both understood the "justification of the ungodly" (Rom 4:5; 5:6) he had experienced and hoped through Christ to attain the resurrection of the dead (cf. Phil 3:11, 20-21). Within these eschatological perspectives he saw himself obligated to take his gospel of justification beyond Rome to Spain. Not only does the discourse about the "demon-stration" of God's righteousness in his installation of Christ as the "place of atonement" (Rom 3:25) acquire its comprehensive overtones within this framework, it also becomes clear why the apostle cannot and will not view justification and the final judg-ment as detached from one another. The Christ of Romans 4:25, who was delivered up for us by God and was raised for our justi-

---

[27]For the identification of Paul himself with the κατέχων compare Cullmann's es-say "Der eschatologische Charakter des Missionsauftrags und des apostolischen Selbstbewußtseins bei Paulus," in *Vorträge und Aufsätze 1925-1962*, ed. K. Fröhli-ch (Tübingen: Mohr Siebeck; Zürich: Zwingli, 1966), pp. 305-36, and P. Stuhlma-cher, *Biblische Theologie des Neuen Testaments II* (Göttingen: Vandenhoeck & Ruprecht, 1999), pp. 54-59.

fication in accordance with Isaiah 53:10-12, is for Paul the living advocate of believers before the judgment throne of God; since his exaltation he intercedes for them unto the Last Judgment (cf. Rom 8:34). He is also the end-time Deliverer who by his appearance in Zion will deliver "all Israel" from its sins and thereby fulfill the promises of salvation given to the people of God (cf. Rom 11:26-32).

4. Conclusion

When Krister Stendahl began to lay the foundation for the new perspective, Ernst Käsemann countered that Paul's doctrine of justification cannot be reduced simply to a plea for the soteriological equality of Gentiles with Jews. Rather, for Paul, "the issue in justification is none other than the kingdom of God that Jesus preached. . . . God's Basileia is the content of the Pauline doctrine of justification."[28] This view can in fact be confirmed from the perspective of Paul's mission. For the apostle, the righteousness of God, the Christ of God, the people of God and the kingdom of God all belong inseparably together. In holding them together Paul thought and taught as a converted Jew whom the exalted Christ had enlisted in the service of worldwide preaching of the gospel of God's kingdom. The justification of individuals before God's judgment throne is the soteriological climax of the event of justification but not its goal. This τέλος lies in the achievement of God's justice in heaven and on earth, that is, in the reconciliation of the cosmos and the establishment of the βασιλεία τοῦ θεοῦ (cf. 1 Cor 15:28).

---

[28]Käsemann, *Paulinische Perspektiven*, p. 133; the German text reads: "in der Rechtfertigung (geht es) um nichts anderes als um die von Jesus verkündigte Gottesherrschaft."

Pauline Eschatology
fits into the double frame
of OT-Jewish expectation of the kingdom of Zion for Israel and all nations
(Is 2:2-4; 28:16; Ps 87; Dan 7; 11Q 05, XII 1-15)
and
early Christian expectation of the restoration of the βασιλεία τῷ Ἰσραήλ after
the completion of the apostolic mission of all nations (Mt 28:16-20; Acts 1:6; 3:20).
According to 1 Corinthians 15:20-28 the βασιλεία is accomplished in three stages:

I. Mission, vicarious death, resurrection and exaltation of Jesus Christ
(Gal 4:4; 1 Cor 15:20,23; Rom 1:3-4; 3:24-26; 4:25; 8:3; Phil 2:6-9; Col 1:15-20)
The exalted Christ
commissions the apostles with the mission to all nations (Mt 28:16-20),
calls Paul to be his minister to the Gentiles (Gal 1:16; Rom 1:5; 11:13; 15:15-24)
and makes him the κατέχων in bringing up the Day of the Lord (2 Thess 2:5-7).
The new people of God from Jews and Gentiles is gathered by the apostolic mission
(baptism of believers [Rom 6], foundation of congregations [1 Cor 3:10-11],
celebration of the Eucharist with the prayer: "μαραναθά" [1 Cor 10:16-17; 16:22]).
According to Mark 13:10 (Mt 24:14) the completion of the apostolic mission leads to

II. The second coming (παρουσία) of Christ in power and heavenly glory
The παρουσία is connected with
resurrection, acceptance, transformation and participation of the believers
in Christ's kingdom
(1 Thess 2:19; 4:13-17; 2 Thess 1:7-10; 2:1; 1 Cor 15:23, 51-52; 2 Cor 3:18; Rom 5:17),
the presentation of the community (bride) to Christ (bridegroom)
(2 Cor 11:2; Eph 5:26-27),
and the submission of the rulers and authorities to Christ (Col 2:15).
After these events follows

III. The End (τὸ τέλος)
It encloses
the Last Judgment (according to the law) on all living and dead through Christ
(Rom 2:5, 16; 14:7-12; 1Cor 11:32; 2 Cor 5:10; Col 3:6; Eph 5:6),
the final justification and glorification of all who believe in Christ
(Gal 5:5; Rom 4:25; 8:31-39),
the salvation of "all Israel" by the redeemer (= Christ), coming out of Zion
(Rom 11:26),
the judgment of the κόσμος and the fallen angels through the saints (1 Cor 6:2-3),
the annihilation of Satan and death (Rom 16:20; 1 Cor 15:26),
the revelation of the children of God in glory,
and the liberation of the κτίσις from the δουλεία τῆς φθορᾶς (Rom 8:19-21).

When all creatures confess, "Κύριος Ἰησοῦς Χριστός" (Phil 2:10-11),
the reconciliation of all things to God is completed (Col 1:20).
Christ will hand over of the kingdom to God (1 Cor 15:24, 28),
and by this act the promised βασιλεία is established:

The one God is "all in all" amid his (re)new(ed) creation (1 Cor 15:28)

Three

THE PROCESS OF
JUSTIFICATION

T he great saving work of justification that the one God real-
izes through Christ Jesus for the sake of Jews and Gentiles as
well as the whole cosmos is best understood by following Paul's
own train of thought. We should avoid subordinating it immedi-
ately to the typical questions of Western justification theology.
For as soon as one does that, one runs into the dead-end of
Anselm's satisfaction theory of the atonement and justification,
underestimates or overestimates Luther's urgent quest for the
gracious God, or gets caught up in the theologically controversial question of the relationship of faith and works. But if we follow Paul, these usual questions fade into the background and
suppressed or forgotten perspectives on the event of justification come once again to the fore.

1. Justification in and Through Christ Jesus
For Paul, *the central figure in the process of justification is Christ*

Jesus. In and through him God effected justification and atonement for Jews and Gentiles. Moreover, Jesus will keep on working to put the βασιλεία τοῦ θεοῦ into effect until the final judgment is accomplished. In 1 Corinthians 1:30 Paul stresses that Christ "became for us wisdom from God, and righteousness and sanctification and redemption." In 2 Corinthians 5:19 he adds that "God was in Christ, reconciling the world to himself, not counting their trespasses against them, and entrusting the message of reconciliation to us" (NRSV modified). In 2 Corinthians 5:21 he continues: "[God] made him who knew no sin to be sin (or rather, a sin offering) on our behalf, so that we might become the righteousness of God in him." This christological line of reasoning is taken up in Romans. God has effected through Christ Jesus the redemption needed by all sinners for salvation. As a demonstration of his saving righteousness God publicly installed Jesus as the ἱλαστήριον or "place of atonement," which is effective through Christ's own blood (Rom 3:24-26). God handed Jesus over to death for our trespasses and raised him for our justification (Rom 4:25). He sent him as a sin offering in order to destroy sin and make us doers of his righteous requirements (Rom 8:3-4). In giving up his own Son for us, God really gave us everything (cf. Rom 8:32). The risen Christ represents us by his intercession before God's throne (cf. Rom 8:34), and he will deliver all Israel from its sins when he appears from Zion and establishes God's kingdom (cf. Rom 11:26). According to Paul, in the mission, death, resurrection and dominion of Christ the one God puts into effect his own saving righteousness. This creates salvation and welfare for Jews, Gentiles and the creation as a whole. *Therefore in and through Christ Jesus, God is the gracious God for all who believe.* Paul places the greatest value upon this knowledge, and it determines his understanding of justification.

2. Atonement and Reconciliation

The representatives of the new perspective propagate afresh the old two-part analysis of Pauline soteriology in terms of a juristic stream and a participatory stream, already proposed by William Wrede and above all by Albert Schweitzer. But this distinction becomes superfluous as soon as we notice Paul's own clear connection between justification, atonement and reconciliation and furthermore recall that Christ Jesus is for Paul always a corporate, representative figure, even as the Messiah and the Son of Man are.

2.1 As 2 Corinthians 5:16-21 and Romans 3:24-26; 4:25; 5:1-11 show, justification, atonement, reconciliation and new creation have the most intimate connection for Paul. In fact, these motifs begin to overlap as early as Second Isaiah (cf. Is 43:3-4, 18-19; 50:8; 53:10-12; 65:17),[1] and the same thing occurs in the Qumran texts. We see that 1QS 11:11-15 (see above) functions like a prelude to Romans 5:1-11, for it says that God demonstrates his righteousness and mercy by delivering sinners characterized by the sins of the flesh, by granting them access to himself and by making atonement for their sins by grace. In the Jesus tradition, justification, atonement and the forgiveness of sins are just as closely bound together as in Qumran. Sufficient proof is found in the various sayings of Jesus. On the one hand are the parable of the Pharisee and the Tax Collector (cf. Lk 18:9-14), and the sayings of Jesus concerning the ransom necessary in the final judgment but impossible for humans to provide (cf. Mk 8:37 par.). Then there is also Jesus' own readiness to surrender his life in death as a ransom for Israel (cf. Mk 10:45 paralleled with Is 43:3). The words of institution at the Lord's Supper have a

---

[1]Compare Gregory K. Beale, "The Old Testament Background of Reconciliation in 2 Corinthians 5—7 and Its Bearing on the Literary Problem of 2 Corinthians 6:14—7:1," *NTS* 35 (1989): 550-51.

similar ring to them (cf. Mk 14:22, 24).

2.2 Even before the call of Paul to be an apostle, the members of the early church made these Jesus sayings their own and interpreted his death on the cross in terms of atonement theology. This is shown not only by the Last Supper tradition but also by the early christological formulas that Paul cites in 1 Corinthians 15:3-5, 2 Corinthians 5:21, Romans 3:25-26 and Romans 4:25. Especially interesting for our investigation is the fact that statements about atonement and justification intersect in these formulas. Jesus' vicarious death is interpreted in them not only from the Suffering Servant tradition in Isaiah 53:10-12, but also from the ransom or exchange tradition in Isaiah 43:3-4 and the sin offering tradition in Leviticus 4, 16. God demonstrates his own saving righteousness by delivering his Christ to death on Golgatha "for the many," by making atonement for their sins and by opening to them a new being in his presence through the forgiveness of sins.

2.3 Paul uses the atonement tradition to make clear the way in which believers share in Jesus' atoning death.

2.3.1 When Isaiah 53:10-12 stands in the background of Paul's christological texts, as it does in Galatians 1:4; 2 Corinthians 5:21; Romans 4:25; 5:8; and 8:34, then the point is that Christ effects justification for sinners as the vicariously Suffering Servant. He bore their iniquities and punishment vicariously and went to death for them while they were still ungodly (cf. Rom 4:25; 5:6-8). Because God made him the bearer of the sins of the many, these many are freed from their sins and may share the righteousness of Christ (cf. 2 Cor 5:21). For our justification Christ was raised from the dead, and now he intercedes for us before God. Taken together, Romans 4:25 and 8:34 give a wide eschatological span to christology: On Good Friday, Christ was delivered up to death by God, and since Easter he makes his death effective before God's judgment throne on behalf of all who confess him as Lord (cf. Rom 10:9-11). If they remain true to him, he remains their advocate until the final judgment so that nothing and no one will be able to separate them from the love of God shown them in Christ Jesus (cf. Rom 8:38-39). Jesus Christ is the living guarantor of believers' justification from Easter until the end of this world.

2.3.2 On the other hand, when Paul's christological texts are stamped by the sin offering tradition or the Day of Atonement tradition in Leviticus 16, as in the case of 2 Corinthians 5:21;[2] Romans 3:24-26; 8:3; and Ephesians 5:2, then the soteriological statements gain added contours. According to Romans 3:24, sinners regain through the redemption that God has effected for them in Christ the glory that they have lacked since Adam's fall (cf. Rom 3:23). If one accepts Hartmut Gese's fundamental insight that atonement "is coming to God by passing through the sentence of death,"[3] then one can say that Christ has passed through the death sentence for sinners and that they have gone with him.[4] By surrendering his blood to God vicariously for them, he provided forgiveness of their sins and new access to God (cf. Rom 3:25-26; 5:1-2). Because they have received forgive-

---

[2]In 2 Corinthians 5:21 the interpretation of Christ's death from Isaiah 53 and the tradition of the sin offering intersect.

[3]Hartmut Gese, "The Atonement," in *Essays on Biblical Theology* (Minneapolis: Augsburg, 1981), pp. 93-116.

[4]In the rite of atonement, "atonement takes place through the sacrifice of the life of a blameless animal which, by a laying on of hands, is *identified* with the one bringing the sacrifice" (ibid., p. 106, italics mine). According to 2 Corinthians 5:21, God himself made his Son the sin offering for the believers; that is, he identified the blameless Christ with the sinners, let him bear their iniquities, suffer death and gain eternal life vicariously for them. So the believers really participate in the death and resurrection of Christ, and Paul can say for them and himself in Galatians 2:20: "It is no longer I who live, but it is Christ who lives in me. And the life I now live in the flesh I live by faith in the Son of God, who loved me and gave himself for me." The beginning of this new existence "in Christ" is baptism (see the text above).

ness of their sins in and through Christ, they are new creatures in him (cf. 2 Cor 5:17). According to Romans 6, the gospel of the justification of sinners through the atoning death of Christ gives baptism its precise sacramental sense: the event of baptism is the event of justification. By confessing Christ as Lord and Savior (cf. Rom 6:17 with 1 Cor 15:3-5 and Rom 10:9-10) and by being baptized in his name, the baptized gain a share in his death on the cross and in the power of his new life. Through Christ's sacrifice they are freed from slavery to sin and are sanctified. Henceforth they are his property and are placed in the service of righteousness, which is God's will. Justification and sanctification are bound together and condition each other.

2.4 If one sees and acknowledges these traditio-historical connections, then the separation of juristic and participatory aspects in the apostle's doctrine of salvation becomes superfluous. This supposed distinction is dealing with two *inseparable* sides of the same process of justification effected by God in and through his Christ, whose legal ground lies in the atoning death of Jesus on Golgotha. Because God himself in his Son was and remains active in this atoning death, the enmity of the flesh against God is overcome through the death of Christ, and room is made in people for the love of God (cf. Rom 5:5).

3. The Realization of Justification

The special feature of the doctrine of justification, or δικαίωσις as Paul presents it in Romans, is that the apostle helps us understand comprehensively what this δικαίωσις means. In justification God acts as creator and gracious judge, sending his Son for the salvation of Gentiles and Jews as well as of the whole creation.

3.1 The apostle introduces his teaching in Romans 1:18—3:20 by showing that the ultimate horizon of justification lies in the final judgment. He makes it clear that no Jew or Gentile can hope to be accepted in the final judgment on the basis of his or her own righteous deeds. Against this background Paul shows in Romans 3:21-30 that God himself by his grace has provided the legal basis for the justification of Jews and Gentiles in the atoning death of Jesus. God demonstrates his saving righteousness by justifying every person who believes in Jesus (cf. Rom 3:26, 30) on the basis of the atonement accomplished on Golgotha. Yet grace does not take precedence over justice in justification. Rather, justification is an event of holy justice in which *the fatal difference between sin and God's holiness is not blurred but overcome.* Sinners are justified because God's own Son died on the cross an accursed death, to which sinners themselves would need to be sentenced as soon as their iniquities were discovered in the final judgment. Because Christ went to death for them vicariously, they are spared the death sentence and may rather share in the dominion of Christ (cf. Rom 5:17). According to Paul not only sinners from among the Gentiles but also all his Jewish contemporaries are to share in justification. Israel was already chosen in Abraham for justification through Christ (cf. Rom 9:5, 8, 11-12 with Rom 11:29-32). Therefore, in the end, Christ will appear from Zion to Israel, which will have remained mostly in unbelief up until then, and will deliver it from the burden of its sins (cf. Rom 11:26-27).

3.2 To what has already been said it must be added from Romans 3:26, 30; 4:5, 17; 5:6 that the event of justification implies an act of *creation.* In justification God is active as the Creator "who calls into existence the things that do not exist" (Rom 4:17). He does this by directing his grace in and through Christ toward those who are nothing before him (cf. 1 Cor 1:28), from Abraham to all those for whom Christ went to his death (cf. Rom 4:5; 5:6). Justification means the establishment of a new being before God (cf. 2 Cor 5:17, 21). Therefore, the controversial and—between Protestants and Catholics since the sixteenth century—much discussed distinction between "imputed" righteousness (which is only credited to the sinner)[5] and "effective" righteousness (which transforms the sinner in his or her being)[6] cannot be maintained from the Pauline texts. Both belong together for the apostle.

3.3 Justification as Paul teaches it has salvation-historical dimensions. This can be seen both christologically and anthropologically.

3.3.1 Christologically, Paul holds that God's work of salvation in and through Christ is historically prior to the faith people place in Jesus Christ. Before sinners could even imagine it, God had already made atonement for them and had made Christ the guarantor of their justification (cf. Rom 4:25; 5:6-8). For Paul the risen Christ must reign until he has put all powers hostile to God in subjection under his feet. Then he can and will hand over the universe pacified to God, his Father (cf. 1 Cor 15:20-28). As far as the cosmos is concerned, this time still lies in the future. But Christ already is exalted to the right hand of God, fights against the powers and is about to overcome them. As the living guarantor of the δικαίωσις of the believers, he intercedes before God's throne for all people who confess him unto and even in the Last Judgment (cf. Rom 8:34). *Through the living and reigning Christ, justification, and with it entrance into God's kingdom, is guaranteed for the believers.*

3.3.2 With regard to the people who share in justification Paul differentiates between *baptismal* and *final justification*. Both presuppose one and the same condition: The ungodly are justified

---

[5]This was (and still is) the Protestant view.
[6]This was (and still is) the Catholic view.

by faith alone for Christ's sake. But for Jewish and Gentile Christians justification nevertheless presents itself as a way that leads from baptism to the final judgment. The point in time at which justification is effectively pronounced to them is the time of their baptismal confession (cf. Rom 10:9-10) and their baptism (cf. 1 Cor 6:11; Rom 6:1-11). With baptism the Christian walks "in newness of life," and this new life begins in the context of the fellowship of believers (cf. Rom 6:4). Baptism makes the baptized men and women Christ's property and incorporates them into his body, that is, the church of Jesus Christ (cf. 1 Cor 12:12-13). As baptized and sanctified members of the body of Christ, Christians lead their lives henceforth in the obedience of faith and expectation of future glory (cf. Rom 5:2-5; 8:18). Baptismal justification grounds their hope of righteousness in the final judgment (cf. Gal 5:5-6). Baptism therefore initiates for Christians a *status of becoming*, and this status lasts until the παρουσία (cf. 1 Thess 4:13-18; 1 Cor 15:51). The church of Jesus Christ on earth participates in its own way in the struggle of its risen Lord in heaven to establish the kingdom of God. But because Christ remains the Lord and reconciler of the baptized from Easter until the final judgment, they can lead their earthly lives confident of Christ's assistance. However, the apostle does not want this assurance of faith to be confused with a security of salvation that forgets or suppresses the fact that God will not be mocked, even by baptized Christians. All Christians, including the apostle himself, must still appear before the judgment seat of God (cf. Gal 6:7; 1 Cor 4:4-5; 10:22; 2 Cor 5:10; Rom 14:10).

4. Justification by Faith Alone

According to Galatians 2:16 and, above all, Romans 3:28 we know that "a person is justified not by the works of the law but (only) through faith in Jesus Christ." These traditional Christian formulas[7] are rightly considered a typical mark of the Pauline doctrine of justification. Paul in Romans 7:12, 14 considers the law of God to be holy, righteous, good and even spiritual. But in view of the requirements of the law, every Jew and Gentile appears in the final judgment as a transgressor (cf. Rom 3:19-20). Therefore, individual performance of the "works prescribed by the law" cannot and will not provide God with any reason to acquit Jews or Gentiles.[8] Paul once considered himself to be a blameless righteous person, but now he only strives for the righteousness that comes from God by grace (cf. Phil 3:4-11). And he does this not only for himself but prototypically for all Jews and Gentiles who believe in Jesus.

4.1 The apostle explains what *faith* is and what type of life it implies with the example of "Abraham our forefather" (Rom 4:1).

4.1.1 Paul's discourse about Abraham in Romans 4 is not accidental. In Galatia Paul's opponents pointed to God's covenant with Abraham, whose sign is circumcision (cf. Gen 17:10-13). They encouraged the Gentile Christians to have themselves circumcised in addition to baptism in order to receive the blessings of the Abrahamic covenant (cf. Jub 1:7, 15ff., 22ff.; 15:1-34). Perhaps they also pointed out that the faith that God had reckoned to Abraham as righteousness was only that which Abraham had already demonstrated by keeping God's "charge, commandments, statutes and laws" (Gen 26:5; cf. Gen 15:6; Sir 44:19-21) and above all by his "binding of Isaac" for sacrifice (cf. Gen 22:9-10 with Jub 18:15ff.; Sir 44:20). Within the New Testament this picture of Abraham's faithfulness is upheld in James 2:14-26 and Hebrews 11:8-10, 17-19. But Paul freed himself from it. He argued on the contrary that Abraham was justified by faith alone

---

[7]For the pre-Pauline origin of these (catechetical) sayings see p. 23 in this manuscript.
[8]Compare Richard H. Bell, *No One Seeks for God* (Tübingen: Mohr Siebeck, 1998).

and that the promise to Abraham applied to believers. Whoever subsequently has himself circumcised in Galatia is returning to slavery under the law (cf. Gal 5:1-3). In Romans 4 the apostle stresses once again that, according to Genesis 15:6, Abraham was justified by God's free electing grace, and his faith was reckoned to him as righteousness; circumcision sealed Abraham's righteousness by faith only as a sign (cf. Rom 4:1-12). Even more pointedly than in Galatians, Paul emphasizes in Romans 4:5-8 that Abraham experienced justification and forgiveness not as a law-abiding righteous person but as one who was *ungodly*. This view can certainly be defended from Genesis 12:1-3.

4.1.2 For Paul, Abraham's faith presents prototypically what it means to believe in the one God who raised Jesus Christ from the dead (cf. Rom 4:23-25). Faith is for Paul the *quintessence of trust in God*. People cannot force this trust to develop by their own efforts, but faith comes from hearing the gospel and is a gift of the Holy Spirit (cf. Gal 3:2; Rom 10:17). All the stages of life in which faith develops, including turning from idols to serve the living and true God and his Son (cf. 1 Thess 1:9-10), confessing Christ as Lord and Savior (cf. 1 Cor 12:3; Rom 10:9) and loving one's neighbor (cf. Gal 5:6; Rom 5:5) are lived out in the power of the Holy Spirit. *Therefore, justification by faith alone is justification by virtue of the grace of God alone, which opens to people the saving way of faith and gives them the power to live this way by the Holy Spirit.*

4.2 What has just been said must be supplemented by two explanatory notes.

4.2.1 The wording of Galatians 2:16 shows quite unambiguously that the expression πίστις Ἰησοῦ Χριστοῦ, which repeatedly appears in Paul's letters (cf. Gal 2:16; 3:22; Phil 3:9; Rom 3:22, 26) does not denote Jesus' own faith or faithfulness but rather our faith *in* Jesus. Somewhat differently from Hebrews 12:2,

Paul never describes Jesus' special relationship with God in terms of "faith" (πίστις) or "believing" (πιστεύειν).[9] The πίστις Ἰησοῦ Χριστοῦ is our human faith in Jesus as Lord and reconciler, and this faith leads to justification (cf. Rom 3:26; 10:9-10).

4.2.2 As much as faith is directed toward the Spirit-filled word of God and is not a meritorious human achievement (cf. Rom 10:17 with 2 Cor 4:6; Gal 3:2), one cannot deny that the apostle describes faith as a human act of obedience (cf. Rom 1:5; 6:16-17; 10:16; 15:18; 16:19). By the example of Abraham he shows that people can and must rely on God's promise by faith, and this faith, "in hope against hope," is the faith that is reckoned as righteousness to Abraham and all other believers (cf. Rom 4:18). Πίστις finds its expression in the Spirit-inspired confession of Jesus Christ as Lord (cf. 1 Cor 12:3; Rom 10:9-10). Moreover, it is active in the ministry of loving one's neighbor, in the keeping of God's commandments and in the righteousness that is God's will (cf. Gal 5:6; 1 Cor 7:19; Rom 6:12-23). Passages such as Philippians 2:12-13; 3:12-16; and 1 Corinthians 9:24-27 show how much Paul believed that faith makes Christians active before God until they have received eternal salvation.

5. Justification and Sanctification

Romans 6:15-23 shows that justification places people in sanctification and the service of righteousness. Through his atoning death on the cross, Christ "sanctified" sinners for their encounter with God (cf. 1 Cor 1:30). For this reason Paul calls the baptized members of the church "the saints" (cf., e.g., 1 Cor 1:2; 6:2; 2 Cor 1:1; Rom 1:7) and thereby differentiates them fundamentally from unbelievers. He requires of them a "walk" worthy of

---

[9]*Pace,* e.g., N. T. Wright, *What Saint Paul Really Said* (Grand Rapids, Mich.: Eerdmans, 1997), p. 127.

their holy being and pleasing to God. He calls this way of life ἁγιασμός, "sanctification" (cf. 1 Thess 4:1-8). In Paul's letters this does not mean something additional to justification, but rather the *atonement-theological consequence and outworking of justification in the lives of believers.*

The call to sanctification in Romans 6:15-23 is a kind of prelude to the extensive exhortation to the Christians of Rome in Romans 12—15. Paul does not offer a closed ethical system but utters *programmatic principles.* Two of them are especially interesting for the theology of justification:

5.1 In the Old Testament and also in Paul's writings the God of justification is the God of mercy. "God has imprisoned all [Jews and Gentiles] in disobedience so that he may be merciful to all" (Rom 11:32). In Romans 12:1-2 Paul appeals to the Christians of Rome to thank this God for his mercies through a living sacrifice consisting of a λογικὴ λατρεία, that is, a spiritual worship service. With this λογικὴ λατρεία the apostle is thinking not only of hymns and prayers, like his Hellenistic Jewish contemporaries, but of the surrender of believers' bodies to God's service. For Paul, the living sacrifice that truly corresponds to God's being and will consists of prayer *and* bodily acts of obedience in everyday living in the world. The apostle proceeds to describe precisely what he means. Now that they are justified and sanctified through Christ, Christians must cease conforming to this world in their thoughts and actions. They should rather be transformed by the renewing of their minds and become genuine thinkers about the will of God in this world. Their lives should no longer be determined by what everyone else thinks and says. With the help of reason that had been taken "captive to the obedience of Christ" (2 Cor 10:5), they should test what is good and what is reprehensible before God and be zealous for the good they have discovered (cf. 1 Thess 5:15; Gal 6:10; Rom 12:9; 13:3).

5.2 Next to his call for bodily acts of obedience Paul places his exhortation to love (cf. Rom 13:8-10). The issue for him in Romans 12:9-13, 15-16; 14:1—15:13 is the behavior of the members of the body of Christ toward each other. They should "accept" one another in their strengths and weaknesses as Christ accepted them to the glory of God (cf. Rom 15:7). But Paul also had in view encounters with people who were far from the church and even persecuted it. In keeping with Christ's own example these people should not be cursed by the church but blessed, and the church should live peaceably with them as far as possible (cf. Rom 12:14, 17-21 with Lk 6:27-35). This double command, both to practice the love of neighbor within the church and to meet differently minded people outside the church in a spirit of love for the enemy, is grounded by Paul in the example of Jesus (cf. Rom 15:1-6). This shows that the bodily worship service in everyday living for which Paul appeals involves the Christian task of witness. As members of the body of Christ, they should testify to their Lord in the still unbelieving world so that unbelievers can see in the life of the church who Christ Jesus is for all people: Savior and Lord, in whom the one God is merciful to all Gentiles and Jews and opens for them the way into his kingdom.

6. Justification and the Final Judgment

Justification (δικαίωσις) means at its core the creative act of justice whereby the one God justifies the individual ungodly person (ἀσεβής) for the sake of Jesus' atoning death. The place of justification is the (final) judgment. Romans 14:10-12 says:

> For we will all stand before the judgment seat of God. For it is written,
>
> "As I live, says the Lord, every
>   knee shall bow to me,

and every tongue shall give
    praise to God!"
So then, each of us will be accountable to God. (NRSV)

It is clear from Romans 13:11-12 that Paul expected the final
judgment in the near future. Christians too will have to appear
before the judgment throne of God, and every individual good or
evil deed that they have done will be weighed. Evil deeds will
bring their punishment and good deeds their reward (cf. Gal 6:2-
5; 2 Cor 5:10). Yet for Christians this will determine not their salvation or damnation but only their position in the kingdom of
God and of his Christ. Christians who have confessed Christ
Jesus and Lord and Savior while on earth may hope and trust in
his advocacy before God's throne in heaven (cf. Rom 8:34); even
when they have failed in what they should have done for him on
earth totally, their final δικαίωσις depends on his vicarious
death and heavenly intercession alone (cf. 1 Cor 3:10-15).
According to Paul only unbelievers are threatened with eternal
destruction.

7. The Salvation of "All Israel"
For Paul, the Jewish Christian, justification and final judgment
were a really big problem when it came to Israel because
(already in his own time) the majority of Jews had refused to
accept the faith in Jesus Christ that Paul preached. Nevertheless, the promise to Abraham was applied to Israel (cf. Gen 12:2-
3; 15:4-5), Israel was promised end-time salvation in Isaiah (cf.
Is 45:17, 25; 59:20), and "all Israel (πας Ἰσραήλ) will be gathered
to the LORD" in the end time according to the Testament of Ben-
jamin 10:11 and Mishna, Sanhedrin 10:1. After stressing in
Romans 1:16 and 2:9 that the gospel and judgment apply "first to
the Jew and then also to the Greek," Paul comes back to the
theme of Israel in Romans 9—11. In these three chapters justifi-

cation receives its special contours from the history of election. According to Romans 9:1-5 Israel has been and remains *distinct* from the Gentiles because of its election privileges. Israel is uniquely privileged among the peoples of the earth, and Paul considers it impossible that God's word of promise to Israel should fail (cf. Rom 9:6). What then? Israel has until now not submitted to God's righteousness in Christ (cf. Rom 10:3) and has refused to obey the gospel that the apostles preach (cf. Rom 10:16). This disobedience provoked the judgment already proclaimed by Moses in Deuteronomy 32:21: Israel itself is far from salvation and must be made jealous of a "non-people" (NJB), the Gentiles, who have obtained the salvation promised to Israel.[10] But God remains inclined toward his disobedient people with a father's outstretched hands even in the hour of his wrath (cf. Rom 10:21). The hardening that God has brought upon Israel occurs within the larger context of his leading the stubborn majority of the people of God to the salvation promised to "all Israel." In Romans 11:25-32 Paul opens up to his readers the *revelation about the salvation of all Israel:*

> So that you may not claim to be wiser than you are, brothers, I want you to understand this mystery: a hardening has come upon part of Israel, until the full number of the Gentiles has come in. And so all Israel will be saved; as it is written,
>   "Out of Zion will come the Deliverer;
>   he will banish ungodliness from Jacob.
>   And this is my covenant with them,
>   when I take away their sins."
> As regards the gospel they are enemies of God for your sake; but as regards election they are beloved, for the sake of their ancestors; for the gifts and the calling of God are irrevocable. Just as

---

[10]For the motive of jealousy in Romans 9—11 compare Richard H. Bell, *Provoked to Jealousy* (Tübingen: Mohr Siebeck, 1994).

you were once disobedient to God but have now received mercy because of their disobedience, so they have now been disobedient in order that, by the mercy shown to you, they too may now receive mercy. For God has imprisoned all in disobedience so that he may be merciful to all. (NRSV)

When the full number of the Gentiles has come in to the congregation of those who will be saved, then the hardening still in effect today will be taken away from Israel, and the people of God as a whole will have the experience that Paul had before Damascus. It will be redeemed from its unbelief by the Christ who appears from Zion[11] and will be received anew into the covenant though the forgiveness of its sins. Not the salvation of the Gentiles alone but the deliverance of all Israel from the hardening of unbelief is the goal of God's history with humanity. Romans 11:32 formulates history's fundamental principle of justification theology: God has imprisoned all Gentiles and Jews in the sin of disobedience so that he may be merciful to all.

8. The Redemption of the Creation from the Curse of Futility

Paul in his teaching about the final events does not rest content with pointing out that Gentiles and Jews will be redeemed through Christ but turns his attention also to the creation (κτίσις), which has been under a curse since Adam's fall (cf. Gen 3:14-24). In Romans 8:18-25 the apostle writes:

I consider that the sufferings of this present time are not worth comparing with the glory about to be revealed to us. For the cre-

---

[11]The appearance of Christ from (Mount) Zion (according to Ps 50:2 [49:2 LXX] and Is 2:2-3; Mic 4:1-2), to which Paul points in Romans 11:26 should not be identified with the Son of God's παρουσία with the clouds of heaven (cf. 1 Thess 4:16-17; Mk 13:26 par.; 14:62 par.) but is an end-time event *after* the second coming of Christ.

ation waits with eager longing for the revealing of the children of
God; for the creation was subjected to futility (ματαιότης), not of
its own will but by the will of the one who subjected it, in hope
that the creation itself will be set free from its bondage to decay
(ἡ δουλεία τῆς φθορᾶς) and will obtain the freedom of the glory of
the children of God. We know that the whole creation has been
groaning in labor pains until now; and not only the creation, but
we ourselves, who have the first fruits of the Spirit, groan
inwardly while we wait for adoption, the redemption of our bodies. For in hope we were saved. Now hope that is seen is not
hope. For who hopes for what is seen? But if we hope for what we
do not see, we wait for it with patience. (NRSV)

The expression "groaning in labor pains" in 8:22 takes up the
Jewish and early Christian expectation that the coming of the
Messiah will be preceded by a time of "messianic birth pangs"
(cf. Is 24:1-6, 16-23 with 26:16-18; Mic 4:9-10; 1 Enoch 62:4; 1QH
3:7-8; Mk 13:8-9 par.). These birth pangs afflict not only humans
but all living creatures. If one keeps this in view, then a clear
answer can be given to the often-posed question of what Paul
means by creation (ἡ κτίσις) in Romans 8:19-22. The apostle is
talking about the whole creation that was subjected to futility
and death with Adam's fall. It will be set free from "futility"
(ματαιότης) and "bondage to decay" (ἡ δουλεία τῆς φθορᾶς) and
will "obtain the freedom of the glory of the children of God" (v.
21). Paul measures this freedom of the children of God against
Daniel 7:22, 27; 12:1-3. These passages speak about the revelation of the Son of Man and of the people he represents, the "holy
ones of the Most High," in end-time glory. The final justification
of believers aims at their glorification (cf. Rom 8:18, 30), and the
nonhuman creation will share this glory. Therefore, in the kingdom of God, headed up by Christ, the redeemed children of God
will be gathered in the midst of a redeemed creation before God
and his Christ.

9. Conclusions

According to everything that we have seen, Paul's doctrine of justification involves not only the salvation of Gentiles and Jews but also the implementation of God's saving righteousness in the whole cosmos. For Paul there can be no doubt about who will put the righteousness of God into effect. He is the Κύριος Ἰησοῦς Χριστός, who has already become wisdom from God and righteousness and sanctification and redemption for believers (cf. 1 Cor 1:30), and who will reign on God's behalf until he has subdued all powers opposing God and has destroyed death (cf. 1 Cor 15:24-28). The Pauline doctrine of justification is the *doctrine about the implementation of God's righteousness through Christ for the entire creation.* Its goal is the establishment of the kingdom of God. This doctrine therefore shows in its own way both that and how God will bring the first and second petitions of the Lord's prayer to their fulfillment (cf. Lk 11:2; Mt 6:10).

Let us therefore be thankful that we have Paul's teaching. If we uphold it in its unabridged form, it will stand us in good stead ecumenically, confessionally and personally.

Four

PAUL & JUDAISM

Testing the New Perspective
DONALD A. HAGNER

Nearly twenty-five years ago E. P. Sanders published his book *Paul and Palestinian Judaism*[1] and began what could well be called a Copernican revolution in Pauline studies.[2] One of the leading advocates of the newer knowledge has dubbed it "The New Perspective on Paul."[3] The revolution, however, is far from complete. Some of us, moreover, continue to believe that the

---

[1] E. P. Sanders, *Paul and Palestinian Judaism* (Philadelphia: Fortress, 1977).
[2] This was followed by a second important book on the subject before us, E. P. Sanders, *Paul, the Law and the Jewish People* (Philadelphia: Fortress, 1983).
[3] This was the title of James D. G. Dunn's Manson Memorial Lecture given at the University of Manchester in November of 1982, published originally in *BJRL* 65 (1983): 95-122, and reprinted together with an "additional note" in Dunn's collected essays *Jesus, Paul and the Law: Studies in Mark and Galatians* (Louisville, Ky.: Westminster John Knox, 1990), pp. 183-214. See too his chapter "Paul and 'Covenantal Nomism,' " in *The Partings of the Ways Between Christianity and Judaism and Their Significance for the Character of Christianity* (London: SCM Press; Philadelphia: Trinity Press, 1991), pp. 117-39; his Henton Davies Lecture, given at Regents Park College, Oxford, "The Justice of God: A Renewed Perspective on Justification by Faith," *JTS* 43 (1992): 1-22; "In Search of Common Ground," in

evidence still points to a geocentric universe—at least so far as Paul's theology is concerned. In this essay I can hardly do justice to the subject, but I propose to analyze briefly the new perspective on Paul and Judaism and also at the same time to offer some critique of it.

1. The fundamental point of the new perspective on Paul has to do not with Paul himself but with the nature of first-century Judaism: contrary to the widespread view held even in leading reference works, *Judaism was not and is not a religion where acceptance with God is earned through the merit of righteousness based on works.* In the same way that Copernicus had his predecessors, this main insight of the new perspective on Paul was adumbrated long before Sanders's book (as he himself readily admits). Moises Silva expresses his surprise—and I share it—at the flurry caused by Sanders's book, since its primary thrust "had been demonstrated in not a few books and was readily accessible in standard works of reference."[4] Silva mentions George Foot Moore's three-volume *Judaism in the First Centuries of the Christian Era.*[5] To that one may add Moore's earlier and well-known article titled "Christian Writers on Judaism," where, like Sanders, he criticizes the work of Ferdinand Weber, as well as Schürer and Bousset, lamenting that legalism "for the last

---

Paul and the Mosaic Law, ed. James D. G. Dunn (Tübingen: Mohr, 1996): 309-34; "Paul and Justification by Faith," in *The Road from Damascus: The Impact of Paul's Conversion on his Life, Thought, and Ministry*, ed. Richard N. Longenecker (Grand Rapids, Mich.: Eerdmans, 1997), pp. 85-101; and now his *Theology of Paul the Apostle* (Grand Rapids, Mich.: Eerdmans, 1998), pp. 334-89. On the pertinent passages in Romans and Galatians, see Dunn's commentaries, respectively in the Word Biblical Commentary (2 vols., 1988) and Black's New Testament Commentary (1993).

[4]Moises Silva, "The Law and Christianity: Dunn's New Synthesis," *WTJ* 53 (1991): 348 (339-53).

[5]The book bears the subtitle "The Age of the Tannaim" and was published in Cambridge, Massachusetts, by Harvard University Press (1927-1930). Silva calls attention 1:110-21, 520-45.

fifty years has become the very definition and the all-sufficient condemnation of Judaism."[6] Further to be mentioned is the work of such scholars as Solomon Schechter,[7] R. Travers Herford,[8] Arthur Marmorstein[9] and especially Claude Goldsmid Montefiore.[10]

To my mind what explains the impact of Sanders's book is that it was the first lengthy and strongly articulated statement of the case in the post-Holocaust era. Thanks to the work of many Jewish writers—and non-Jewish too—people have become sensitized concerning the role of anti-Judaism in nourishing the evil of anti-Semitism. It was a point whose time had come.

2. A second and nearly as important point in the new perspective on Paul is again one that had been made much earlier: contrary to the Reformation understanding of Paul, *justification by faith is not the center of Paul's theology but instead represents a pragmatic tactic to facilitate the Gentile mission.* It will be easily seen how well this works together with the preceding point. If Judaism is not a religion of works-righteousness, then it hardly needs to hear the message of justification by faith, whereas that message makes perfect sense if it was directed solely to the Gentiles.

Although this point is not very important in Sanders's book,

---

[6]George Foot Moore, "Christian Writers on Judaism," *HTR* 14 (1921): 252 (197-254).

[7]Solomon Schechter, *Aspects of Rabbinic Theology* (New York: Macmillan, 1909; reprint, New York: Schocken, 1961).

[8]See especially R. Travers Herford, *Judaism in the New Testament Period* (London: Lindsey, 1928); "The Fundamentals of Religion As Interpreted by Christianity and Rabbinic Judaism," *HJ* 21 (1922-1923): 314-26.

[9]Arthur Marmorstein, *The Doctrine of Merits in Old Rabbinical Literature* (London: Oxford University Press, 1920; reprint, New York: KTAV, 1968).

[10]See, e.g., C. G. Montefiore, "On Some Misconceptions of Judaism and Christianity by Each Other," *JQR* 8 (1896): 193-216; "Jewish Scholarship and Christian Silence," *HJ* 1 (1902-1903): 335-46; *Rabbinic Literature and Gospel Teaching* (London: Macmillan, 1930; reprint, New York: KTAV, 1970).

he does review the arguments of Albert Schweitzer concerning the relatively small importance of justification by faith in Paul's theology, concluding that "they have never been effectively countered."[11] Schweitzer put his conclusion in a typically vivid metaphor: "The doctrine of righteousness by faith is therefore a subsidiary crater, which has formed within the rim of the main crater—the mystical doctrine of redemption through the being-in-Christ."[12] The conclusion concerning the subordinate importance of the doctrine was not even original with Schweitzer, having already been argued at least as early as 1853 by Lipsius and also Sabatier, Lüdemann, Weizsäcker and Wrede.[13] The new perspective on Paul has given new life to this argument.[14]

3. These two main foundations of the new perspective on Paul thus raise again two fundamental questions: What was the nature of first-century Judaism? and What is at the heart of Paul's Christianity? Or, to put the question differently, What was the difference between Saul the Pharisee and Paul the Christian? The answers to these interrelated questions have produced a number of corollary conclusions, and to these we now turn.

3.1 The new perspective on Paul maintains that *Paul's theology has been misunderstood because it has been read through the lenses of Luther and the Reformation.* Luther's rediscovery of the gospel was preceded by an agonizing personal struggle with the prob-

---

[11]Sanders, *Paul and Palestinian Judaism*, p. 440.

[12]Albert Schweitzer, *The Mysticism of Paul the Apostle*, trans. William Montgomery (New York: Seabury, 1931), p. 225.

[13]See the informative article by Ronald Y.-K. Fung, "The Status of Justification by Faith in Paul's Thought: a Brief Survey of a Modern Debate," *Themelios* 6 (1981): 4-11. See too the appendix in Sanders's *Paul and Palestinian Judaism* by Manfred T. Brauch, "Perspectives on 'God's Righteousness' in Recent German Discussion," pp. 523-42.

[14]Compare Krister Stendahl, *Paul Among Jews and Gentiles* (Philadelphia: Fortress, 1976), pp. 1-2.

lem of sin and of attempted self-justification. Such was not the case with Paul, as Philippians 3:6, referring to Paul's background as a Pharisee, indicates: "As to righteousness under the law, [I was] blameless" (NRSV). Since Judaism was not a religion of works-righteousness, Paul did not have to move from legalism to grace, as in the typical Protestant schema.

Proponents of the new perspective on Paul have made much of Krister Stendahl's 1963 article "The Apostle Paul and the Introspective Conscience of the West."[15] It was indeed a groundbreaking article in some ways, anticipating much of the new perspective; yet even its main point had been articulated much earlier. Thomas Walter Manson had already in 1938 written, "The Faith and Works controversy has obtained an undue emphasis through our reading of Paul in the light of the soul-strivings of Luther."[16] For Stendahl, a bishop in the Lutheran Church of Sweden, Luther has now come into disfavor—at least so far as being a guide to the interpretation of Paul's gospel is concerned.[17]

3.2 A further, related corollary in the new perspective argues that *Paul experienced not conversion to a new faith, not a change of religion, but a call and commission to bring the gospel to the Gentiles.* Paul remained a fully faithful Jew throughout his life.[18] This again is not a particularly new claim. Jewish scholars have for

---

[15]Krister Stendahl, "The Apostle Paul and the Introspective Conscience of the West," *HTR* 56 (1963): 199-215; now available in Stendahl, *Paul Among Jews and Gentiles*, pp. 78-96.

[16]Thomas Walter Manson, "Jesus, Paul and the Law," in *Law and Religion*, vol. 3 of Judaism and Christianity, ed. Erwin Isak Jakob Rosenthal (London: Sheldon; New York: Macmillan, 1938; reprint, New York: KTAV, 1969), p. 132 (125-41).

[17]See the especially strong attack on Luther and the "Protestant" understanding of the question in Francis Watson, *Paul, Judaism and the Gentiles: A Sociological Approach*, SNTSMS 56 (Cambridge: Cambridge University Press, 1986), pp. 1-22.

[18]See especially Stendahl's "Call Rather than Conversion," in *Paul Among Jews and Gentiles* (Philadelphia: Fortress, 1976), pp. 7-23. Compare James D. G. Dunn, "'A Light to the Gentiles', or 'The End of the Law'? The Significance of the Damascus Road Christophany for Paul," in *The Glory of Christ in the New Tes-*

some time been engaged in reclaiming Paul for Judaism, arguing not only his enduring Jewishness but also that his task was
in effect that of bringing Judaism to the Gentiles.[19]

3.3 Closely related to the preceding is the conclusion that *Paul's
main concern was the Jewish-Gentile problem, specifically the conversion of the Gentiles, rather than any universal human problem.* That
is, Paul's theological thinking is dominated by the need to defend
the right of the Gentiles to become full members of the people of
God without first becoming Jews. Stendahl again puts it very
clearly when he writes that the "doctrine of justification by faith
was hammered out by Paul for the very specific and limited purpose of defending the rights of Gentile converts to be full and genuine heirs to the promises of God to Israel."[20] This is, of course,
also closely related to the claim of the new perspective noted in
section 2, since it further relativizes the doctrine of justification
by faith.

3.4 A conclusion drawn from a number of the preceding points
is that *Paul had no quarrel with the law (and hence Judaism) per se.*
This has become one of the central tenets of the new perspective
on Paul. If Judaism was a "covenantal nomism," to use Sanders's
nomenclature—that is, a law-centeredness in the context of prior
experience of grace—then Paul could hardly have been unhappy

---

tament: *Studies in Christology in Memory of George Bradford Caird,* ed. L. D. Hurst
and N. T. Wright (Oxford: Clarendon, 1987), pp. 251-66, available now with an
"additional note" in Dunn, *Jesus, Paul and the Law,* pp. 89-107; see too Dunn,
Partings of the Ways, p. 122, and Peter J. Tomson, *Paul and the Jewish Law: Hala-
kha in the Letters of the Apostle to the Gentiles* (Assen: Van Gorcum; Minneapolis:
Fortress, 1990).

[19]For a full account of Jewish scholarship on Paul, see Stefan Meissner, *Die Heim-
holung des Ketzers: Studien zur jüdischen Auseinandersetzung mit Paulus,* WUNT
2.87 (Tübingen: Mohr, 1996); compare Donald A. Hagner, "Paul in Modern Jewish Thought," *Pauline Studies: Essays Presented to Professor F. F. Bruce on his 70th
Birthday,* ed. Donald A. Hagner and Murray J. Harris (Exeter: Paternoster;
Grand Rapids, Mich.: Eerdmans, 1980), pp. 143-65.

[20]Stendahl, *Paul Among Jews and Gentiles,* p. 2.

[handwritten margin note: This doesn't make sense]

with it, even as a Christian. His apparently negative statements concerning the law are therefore dictated solely by the exigencies of the Gentile mission. Paul's "new understanding of the law" is the result of his call to evangelize the Gentiles.[21] Sanders explains Paul's rejection of his earlier faith with these words: "In short, *this is what Paul finds wrong in Judaism: it is not Christianity.*"[22]

[handwritten margin note: what about Jesus?]

3.5 Since he had no quarrel with the law, according to the new perspective, *Paul's arguments against "works of the law" do not concern the issue of righteousness by obedience to the law, but simply Jewish badges of identity that separated Jews from the Gentiles.* Dunn in particular has stressed that "works of the law" refers to "national righteousness."[23] According to him the "boasting" of the Jews that Paul repeatedly criticizes refers not to self-confidence but to "Jewish" confidence.[24]

Dunn has labored hard to defend the interpretation of "works of the law" as the marks of Jewish privilege,[25] tackling first Galatians 2:16 in his new perspective article, then turning to Galatians 3:10-14,[26] and of course the Romans passages in his commentary. Recent monographs on Galatians by John Barclay

---

[21]Ibid., p. 9.

[22]Sanders, *Paul and Palestinian Judaism*, p. 552, emphasis in original.

[23]This phrase (and insight?) is borrowed from N. T. Wright's 1980 Oxford dissertation, "The Messiah and the People of God: A Study in Pauline Theology with Particular Reference to the Argument of the Epistle to the Romans." So far as I can see, Dunn nowhere refers to Wright's 1978 Tyndale New Testament Lecture titled "The Paul of History and the Apostle of Faith," which already articulates key aspects of the new perspective on Paul. The lecture was published in *TB* 29 (1978): 61-88. C. Bryan, in an article without a single mention of Dunn, concludes that the issue in Romans 9:30—10:4 is "that concern with personal and corporate holiness which had characterized the Judaism in which he [Paul] grew up" ("Law and Grace in Paul: Thoughts on E. P. Sanders," *Saint Luke's Journal of Theology* 34 [1991]: 50 [33-52]).

[24]Dunn, "Justice of God," p. 11.

[25]For the similar view of Sanders, see *Paul, the Law, and the Jewish People*, p. 160.

[26]Dunn, "Works of the Law and the Curse of the Law (Gal 3:10-14)," in *Jesus, Paul and the Law*, pp. 215-41. See also James D. G. Dunn, "Yet Once More—'The Works of the Law': A Response," *JSNT* 46 (1992): 99-117.

and Walter Hansen join in the conclusion that the issue in Galatians is not Jewish legalism but national righteousness or the
law in terms of badges of Jewish identity.[27] Francis Watson and
Donald Garlington (who did his research under Dunn) examine
Romans from this perspective and come to similar conclusions.[28]

3.6 It is not far from these conclusions to a final deduc-
tion—one not drawn, however, by all advocates of the new
understanding of Paul. If Judaism is a religion of grace, and
there is nothing wrong with its nomism in Paul's view, and if
Paul's message therefore concerns the Gentiles rather than
the Jews, a natural conclusion is that *the covenantal nomism of
the Old Testament is God's way of salvation for Israel, while the
law-free gospel is God's way of salvation for the Gentiles.* The
pressure toward the so-called two-covenant theory of salvation continues to be a constant factor in Jewish-Christian dialogue today.[29] Four advocates of the new view of Paul who
have also accepted the two-covenant approach are Stendahl,[30]

---

[27]John Barclay, *Obeying the Truth: A Study of Paul's Ethics in Galatians* (Edinburgh:
T & T Clark, 1988), pp. 235-42; Walter Hansen, *Abraham in Galatians: Epistolary
and Rhetorical Contexts*, JSNTSS 29 (Sheffield: JSOT, 1989), pp. 161-62.
[28]Watson, *Paul, Judaism and the Gentiles*, pp. 88-176; Don B. Garlington, *"The Obedience of Faith": A Pauline Phrase in Historical Context*, WUNT 2.38 (Tübingen:
Mohr, 1991). Similar in many ways are Neil Elliott, *The Rhetoric of Romans: Ar-
gumentative Constraint and Strategy and Paul's Dialogue with Judaism*, JSNTSS 45
(Sheffield: JSOT, 1990); and C. Thomas Rhyne, *Faith Establishes the Law*, SBLDS
55 (Chico, Calif.: Scholars Press, 1981).
[29]For shrewd observation of a number of ironies in aspects of the new perspective
on Paul, see R. Barry Matlock, "Almost Cultural Studies? Reflections on the
'New Perspective' on Paul," *Biblical/Cultural Studies: The Third Sheffield Collo-
quium*, JSOTSS 266, ed. J. Cheryl Exum and Stephen D. Moore (Sheffield: Sheffield Academic Press, 1998), pp. 433-59. For a merciless deconstruction of the
new perspective, see Matlock's "Sins of the Flesh and Suspicious Minds: Dunn's
New Theology of Paul," *JSNT* 72 (1998): 67-90. Dunn responds to the latter in
"Whatever Happened to Exegesis? In Response to the Reviews by R. Barry Matlock and D. A. Campbell," *JSNT* 72 (1998): 113-20.
[30]For Stendahl, Paul's gospel was only for the Gentiles. See Stendahl, *Paul Among*

Markus Barth,[31] John G. Gager[32] and Lloyd Gaston.[33] Others, such as Sanders and Dunn,[34] have resisted this conclusion. It is not difficult to see how the various elements of the new perspective on Paul can lead to this appealing, but in my view unbiblical, conclusion.

4. Naturally in this brief review we have not done justice to the strength of the arguments that have been put forward by the advocates of the new perspective on Paul. Our purpose has merely been to note the major assertions in the discussion of Paul and Judaism that blend together to produce that new perspective. It will, of course, be impossible to respond adequately to these arguments in the confines of this essay. But I do want to comment briefly on each of them.

There have been a number of responses to various aspects of the new perspective, as we shall see. Among the more substantial treatments of the whole subject, we may note Stephen Westerholm's *Israel's Law and the Church's Faith: Paul and His Recent Interpreters,*[35] Colin Kruse's *Paul, the Law and Justifica-*

Jews and Gentiles, p. 2.

[31]See Markus Barth's collection of essays titled *The People of God* (Sheffield: JSOT, 1983), where a two-covenant theory is at least implied.

[32]John C. Gager, *The Origins of Anti-Semitism* (Oxford: Oxford University Press, 1983).

[33]See Lloyd Gaston's collected essays in *Paul and the Torah* (Vancouver: University of British Columbia Press, 1987).

[34]Explicitly in Dunn, *Partings of the Ways,* p. 250: "Jewish/Christian dialogue in this area has tended to pose the issue in terms of one covenant or two; and clearly I lean to the 'one covenant' side." Yet his position is very nuanced and it is not always clear how his conclusions are compatible with a one covenant position. Perhaps this explains the word *lean.*

[35]Stephen Westerholm, *Israel's Law and the Church's Faith: Paul and His Recent Interpreters* (Grand Rapids, Mich.: Eerdmans, 1988). See too his "Paul and the Law in Romans 9—11," in *Paul and the Mosaic Law,* ed. James D. G. Dunn (Tübingen: Mohr Siebeck, 1996; Grand Rapids, Mich.: Eerdmans, 2001), pp. 215-37; and "Sinai As Viewed from Damascus: Paul's Reevaluation of the Mosaic Law," in *The Road from Damascus: The Impact of Paul's Conversion on his Life, Thought, and Ministry,* ed. Richard N. Longenecker (Grand Rapids, Mich.: Eerdmans, 1997), pp. 147-65.

tion,[36] and Mark A. Seifrid's *Christ, Our Righteousness: Paul's Theology of Justification.*[37]

We turn first then to the two main points considered in sections 1 and 2.

4.1 Few, if any, will want to deny that what is found in the Old Testament, namely the religion of Israel, is indeed a religion of grace rather than works-righteousness. To say this, however, is not enough. In the postexilic period, beginning with the prototypical scribe Ezra, there was understandably a turning to the law with a new intensity of commitment. The exile was widely perceived as the result of Israel's failure to keep the law. In this new development, which constitutes the beginning of Judaism, it is hardly surprising that the law assumed central importance. Judaism is, of course, in continuity with the Old Testament, and grace was not necessarily occluded by the heightened emphasis on the law. But that it was overshadowed by the new emphasis on the law seems highly probable to me.

Heikki Räisänen, it should be noted, has adamantly continued to argue against Sanders and Dunn that Paul *does* portray Judaism as legalistic. Then, however, he asserts that Judaism could not have been legalistic (an a priori conclusion dependent

---

[36]Colin Kruse, *Paul, the Law and Justification* (Leicester: Apollos, 1996; Peabody, Mass.: Hendrickson, 1997).

[37]Mark A. Seifrid, *Christ, Our Righteousness: Paul's Theology of Justification,* New Studies in Biblical Theology 9 (Downers Grove, Ill.: InterVarsity Press, 2000). Adapted from this book is Seifrid's "The 'New Perspective on Paul' and Its Problems," *Themelios* 25 (2000): 4-18. Also worthy of mention is the brief but insightful excursus on Romans 3:20 ("Paul, 'Works of the Law,' and First-Century Judaism") in Douglas Moo's commentary, *The Epistle to the Romans,* NICNT (Grand Rapids, Mich.: Eerdmans, 1996), pp. 211-17. Much of Moo's helpful and insightful review article, "Paul and the Law in the Last Ten Years" *(SJT* 40 [1987]: 287-307) is also relevant to the subject of the present article. See also R. Barry Matlock, "A Future for Paul?" *Auguries: The Jubilee Volume of the Sheffield Department of Biblical Studies,* JSOTSS 269, ed. David J. A. Clines and Stephen D. Moore (Sheffield: Sheffield Academic Press, 1998), pp. 144-83.

on Sanders) and that therefore Paul is responsible for a distortion of first-century Judaism, being concerned only to defend and promote the Gentile mission.[38]

It is a good question to what extent the rabbis or proto-rabbis of the first century assumed and articulated the grace that was foundational to the religion of their Old Testament forebears. Apart from the notorious problem of what in the rabbinic literature can be taken as going back to or reflecting the situation of the first century, one must note not only the lack of systematic thinking but the presence of (and delight in!) contradictory opinions. It is furthermore the case that there *are* plenty of legalistic-sounding statements in the rabbinic literature. Klyne Snodgrass gently points this out when he writes, "There is an emphasis on weighing good deeds against bad in some writings and on the keeping of ledger books in others, and this cannot be dismissed as easily as Sanders would like."[39] Such statements collected for example in Billerbeck and Kittel do exist; the just criti-

---

[38]Heikki Räisänen, *Paul and the Law* (Tübingen: Mohr, 1987), pp. xxvi-xxix.

[39]Klyne Snodgrass, "Justification by Grace—to the Doers: An Analysis of the Place of Romans 2 in the Theology of Paul," *NTS* 32 (1986): 78 (72-93). Compare Robert H. Gundry: "If we weigh their emphases—quite a different impression may be gained, an impression of Palestinian Judaism as centered on works-righteousness and Paul's theology as centered on grace" ("Grace, Works, and Staying Saved in Paul," *Bib* 66 [1985]: 6 [1-38]). Although Jacob Neusner agrees with Sanders's portrayal of Judaism, a comment he makes in his review of Sanders's book points in the same direction: "An apology for Rabbinic Judaism bypassing the whole of the *halakhic* corpus which constitutes its earliest stratum is cosmically irrelevant to the interpretation of Rabbinic Judaism, therefore to the comparison of that system to others in its own culture" ("Comparing Judaisms," *History of Religions* 18 [1978-1979]: 187 n. 14 [177-91]). This article is taken up in slightly altered form within "The Use of the Later Rabbinic Evidence for the Study of Paul," in *Approaches to Ancient Judaism*, ed. William Scott Green (Chico, Calif.: Scholars Press, 1980), 2:43-63, where the above quotation has been moved from the footnote to the text. Sanders responds to Neusner and to the similar criticisms of Anthony J. Saldarini (in his review of Sanders's book [*JBL* 98 (1979): 299-303]) in an article that follows Neusner's "Puzzling Out Rabbinic Judaism" (65-79).

cism is that these works cite only these texts and not others that point in a different direction.

In a thorough survey of the pertinent materials, Friedrich Avemarie has demonstrated that the rabbinic soteriology contains two different—indeed, contrary—models, one based on the election of Israel, the other on the deeds of the individual. In different places one or the other can come to expression in apparently absolute terms, and it is impossible finally to give priority to either.[40] It is thus not a matter of *either* grace *or* merit but the two together in an unresolved tension.

Earlier Jewish scholars were ready to allow the very strong emphasis on works among the rabbis. Solomon Schechter cites the famous paradox attributed to R. Akiba (Aboth 3.20): "The world is judged by grace, and yet all is according to the amount of work."[41] Israel Abrahams refers to the Jewish doctrine as "something like the *synergism* of Erasmus, which, as his opponents saw, was radically opposed to the Pauline theory of grace." After citing the same logion of Akiba, he adds that "the antinomy [of grace and works] is the ultimate doctrine of Pharisaism."[42] Even if we allow that the emphasis on works has to do

---

[40]Friedrich Avemarie, "Erwählung und Vergeltung: Zur optionalen Struktur rabbinischer Soteriologie," *NTS* 45 (1999): 108-26; *Torah und Leben: Untersuchungen zur Heilsbedeutung der Torah in der frühen rabbinischen Literatur* (Tübingen: Mohr Siebeck, 1996); "Bund als Gabe und Recht," in *Bund und Tora: Zur theologischen Begriffsgeschichte in alttestamentlicher, frühjüdischer und urchristlicher Tradition*, ed. Friedrich Avemarie and Hermann Lichtenberger (Tübingen: Mohr Siebeck, 1996), pp. 163-216.

[41]Schechter, *Aspects of Rabbinic Theology*, p. 15. Schechter calls attention to the variant reading, "and *not* according to the amount of work," and the interesting fact that the difference was of no real concern to the commentators.

[42]Israel Abrahams, *Studies in Pharisaism and the Gospels*, 1st series (Cambridge: Cambridge University Press, 1917; reprint, New York: KTAV, 1967), p. 146. For a fascinating and illuminating discussion of the subject from a Jewish point of view, see C. G. Montefiore's long comment on Matthew 7:24-27 in *Rabbinic Literature and Gospel Teachings* (London: Macmillan, 1930; reprint, New York: KTAV, 1970), pp. 154-201. For the explanation of Judaism as a *synergistic* nom-

with "staying in" rather than "getting in," as Sanders maintains, we are still be confronted with a decided preoccupation with works, a preoccupation that by its very nature makes for human insecurity and thus prepares a promising ground for the nurture of legalistic tendencies. The line between getting in and staying in can furthermore become a thin one that tends to disappear.[43]

Since the rabbis can also speak of grace and since a religion should always be judged by its best representatives, is it not fair to admit that Judaism is a religion of grace and not one where God's favor is earned through righteous works? This seems true, at least at the theoretical level. In its best theology, Judaism *is* a religion of grace. Often, however, its gracious foundations are tacitly assumed[44] and often the law takes a place of overwhelming priority. It is not surprising if a religion whose heart lies in praxis rather than theory (theology), a religion dominated by

ism, see Timo Eskola, "Paul, Predestination and 'Covenantal Nomism': Reassessing Paul and Palestinian Judaism," *JSJ* 28 (1997): 390-441; see too his monograph *Theodicy and Predestination in Pauline Soteriology,* WUNT 2.100 (Tübingen: Mohr Siebeck, 1998); and "*Avodat Israel* and the 'Works of the Law' in Paul," in *From the Ancient Sites of Israel: Essays on Archaeology, History and Theology in Memory of Aapeli Saarisalo,* ed. Timo Eskola and E. Junkkaala (Helsinki: Theological Institute of Finland, 1998), pp. 175-97.

[43]C. F. D. Moule points this out in the following words: "Maintenance of it [the covenantal relation] in Judaism by 'works' . . . does seem to me not far off from the 'legalism' . . . which Dr Sanders holds that Paul is not attacking. . . . I am asking whether 'covenantal nomism' itself is so far from implicit 'legalism'" ("Jesus, Judaism, and Paul," in *Tradition and Interpretation in the New Testament: Festschrift E. Earle Ellis,* ed. Gerald F. Hawthorne and Otto Betz [Tübingen: Mohr Siebeck; Grand Rapids, Mich.: Eerdmans, 1987], p. 48 [43-52]).

[44]Thomas F. Best has called attention to this problem: "His [Sanders's] insistence that the covenant-concept is central in the rabbinic literature, though virtually unmentioned, depends on the ability to demonstrate that it was in fact in the background of the documents as the inescapable presupposition of their discussion on matters of ritual purification, means of atonement, and the definition of 'work.' But in other areas he uses the argument from silence to cut the other way: Since a treasury of merits is not mentioned in the literature, such a concept was not a part of Judaism in this period." See Best, "The Apostle Paul and E. P. Sanders: The Significance of Paul and Palestinian Judaism," *RestQ* 25 (1982): 72-73 (65-74).

nomism, where the covenant is more presupposed than articulated, inadvertently produces followers who fall into a legalistic
mode of existence. This may explain the "exception" of 4 Ezra
(cf. 2 Baruch) with its clear legalism, which Sanders does not
deny.[45] Thus, it is not hard to believe that during the time of
Jesus and Paul there were many who—against the best understanding of their faith—had fallen into legalism, against which
both Jesus and Paul had therefore to contend.[46] A covenantal
nomism will only remain "covenantal" where very deliberate
and explicit measures are taken to guard it as such; there will
otherwise be a natural human tendency toward legalism. There
have been many instances where the experience of Christian
congregations substantiates this. The situation of the Jews in the
postexilic period, suffering under Roman rule, naturally heightened the emphasis on the performance of the law.

It is therefore not at all evident, in my opinion, that there
were no Jews around in the time of Paul who corresponded to
the legalists attacked by him in the traditional understanding of
works-righteousness. I am reminded of the wry remark of C. K.
Barrett: "He is a bold man who supposes that he understands
first-century Judaism better than Paul did."[47]

---

[45]Sanders, *Paul and Palestinian Judaism*, pp. 421-22.

[46]So too, Silva, "Law and Christianity," p. 349: "Sanders is insensitive to the fact
that both in [Christian theologians of] medieval times and in Judaism many lay
people may indeed have perceived salvation along those [legalistic] lines."
Among other scholars who argue that first-century Judaism was legalistic, compare Hans Hübner, "Pauli Theologiae Proprium," *NTS* 26 (1979-1980): 445-73;
and Thomas R. Schreiner, "'Works of Law' in Paul," *NovT* 33 (1991): 217-44.
Schreiner continues to hold to the so-called Reformation understanding of Paul:
"What he [Paul] opposes is the delusion of those who think they can earn merit
before God by their obedience to the law, even though they fail to obey it" (p.
244). See his *The Law and Its Fulfillment: A Pauline Theology of Law* (Grand Rapids, Mich.: Baker, 1993).

[47]C. K. Barrett, *Paul: An Introduction to His Thought* (Louisville, Ky.: Westminster
John Knox, 1994), p. 78.

4.2 It is, of course, debatable whether justification by faith is the "center" of Paul's theology. What is more important for our purposes is whether justification by faith is *important* for Paul, indeed, to the extent that it is more than a ploy merely to advance the Gentile mission, but a doctrine indispensable even for the salvation of the Jews. I am persuaded by those who have argued that the most fundamentally important element in Paul's theology is that the work of Christ inaugurates an eschatological turning point in history.[48] Within that overarching *Heilsgeschichte* framework (which to my mind provides continuity between Jesus and Paul), justification assumes an especially important place.[49] This is seen especially, of course, in the closely argued soteriological sections of Galatians and Romans, but it is also found in the Corinthian letters,[50] as well as in Philippians and, were we allowed

---

[48]To my mind Neusner is entirely correct when he points to this as constituting the real difference between Paul and the perspective of the Pharisees: the Christian view presupposes "an ontology quite distinct from that of the cult, an ontology which centers, as I just said, on a profoundly disruptive historical event, one which has shattered all that has been regular and orderly. So far as history stands at the center of being, so that the messiah and the conclusion of history form the focus of interest, the ontological conception of Christianity scarcely intersects with that of Pharisaism" ("The Use of the Later Rabbinic Evidence for the Study of First-Century Pharisaism," in *Approaches to Ancient Judaism: Theory and Practice,* ed. William Scott Green [Missoula, Mont.: Scholars Press, 1978], p. 225 [215-28]).

[49]See Ernst Käsemann, "Justification and Salvation History in the Epistle to the Romans," in *Perspectives on Paul,* trans. Margaret Kohl (London: SCM Press, 1971), pp. 60-78. In Käsemann's view, "it has rightly been repeatedly noticed that the apostle's message of justification is a fighting doctrine, directed against Judaism" (p. 70). Compare Rudolf Bultmann: "Still more would he [a Jew] contradict the proposition that *justification by works of the Law and justification by divine grace appropriated in man's faith exclude each other.* But that is the decisive thesis of Paul: 'for Christ is the end of the law, that every one who has faith may be justified' (Rom. 10:4); i.e., 'Christ means the end of the Law; he leads to righteousness everyone who has faith' " (*Theology of the New Testament,* trans. Kendrick Grobel [London: SCM Press, 1952], 1.263).

[50]See Fung, "Justification by Faith in 1 & 2 Corinthians," *Pauline Studies,* pp. 246-61.

to appeal to it, Ephesians.[51]

J. Gresham Machen's response to Wrede on this very point is worth quoting in full:

> The real reason why Paul was devoted to the doctrine of justification by faith was not that it made possible the Gentile mission, but rather that it was true. Paul was not devoted to the doctrine of justification by faith because of the Gentile mission; he was devoted to the Gentile mission because of the doctrine of justification by faith.[52]

Without question, the doctrine of justification by faith in and through the finished work of Christ made the Gentile mission a possibility. But from Paul's perspective it also made possible the salvation of the Jews. Justification by faith is addressed to both Jew and Gentile because it addresses a universal human need.[53]

5. I press on now to respond, albeit briefly, to the corollaries mentioned in section 3.

5.1 Although justification by faith is often criticized for being concerned only with the salvation of the individual, as in the crisis of an individual over the problem of sin—on the model of

---

[51]For an excellent discussion of the subject, see John Reumann, *'Righteousness' in the New Testament: 'Justification'* in the United States Lutheran-Roman Catholic Dialogue, with responses by Joseph A. Fitzmyer and Jerome D. Quinn (Philadelphia: Fortress; New York: Paulist, 1982). Reumann notes his continuing conviction concerning "the soundness of the Reformation choice in this perspective" and that "while righteousness/justification is by no means the only way to express Paul's message, the case for regarding it as the central one remains a persuasive one" (p. 108).

[52]J. Gresham Machen, *The Origin of Paul's Religion* (London: Hodder & Stoughton, 1921), pp. 278-79. I owe this quotation to Fung, "Status of Justification by Faith," p. 8.

[53]For an excellent discussion of this whole question, see K. T. Cooper, "Paul and Rabbinic Soteriology: A Review Article," *WTJ* 44 (1982): 123-39, esp. 136ff. As Cooper says, "Paul's soteriology forms a much more specific and pointed contrast to covenantal nomism than Sanders has observed" (p. 136). On the whole matter, we may look forward with anticipation to a two-volume work titled *Justification and Variegated Judaism*, ed. D. A. Carson, P. T. O'Brien and M. Seifried (Tübingen: Mohr Siebeck; Grand Rapids, Mich.: Baker, 2001).

Luther—properly understood, it has corporate and cosmic aspects too.[54] Leaving that point aside, however, and coming to the personal level, I want to make the following observations. In my opinion we read too much into Paul's statement in Philippians 3:6: "as to righteousness under the law [I was] blameless *(amemptos)"* (NRSV), when we conclude from it that Paul was fully pleased with both the law and his performance of it. He indicates here only that by the standards of practicing Pharisees he had an exceptionally good performance record (cf. Gal 1:13-14).[55] It is certainly not anything in the end that he as a Jew felt he could rely upon. Quite the contrary, all his credentials and efforts amounted to worthless rubbish, as he goes on to say, putting him in complete dependence upon Christ: "not having a righteousness of my own that comes from the law, but one that comes through faith in Christ" (Phil 3:8-9 NRSV).

Timo Laato has shown how Paul is critical of Jewish soteriology on anthropological grounds.[56] Laato indicates how, unlike

---

[54]Compare Reumann, *"Righteousness"* in the New Testament, pp. 73-74: "Righteousness/justification in Paul has a cosmic side, relating God's faithfulness and saving righteousness to all creation, within a new covenant setting. This emphasis is utterly necessary alongside the individual emphasis." See especially Ernst Käsemann, "Justification and Salvation History in the Epistle to the Romans," in *Perspectives on Paul* (Philadelphia: Fortress, 1971), pp. 32-59; and Peter Stuhlmacher, *Reconciliation, Law, and Righteousness: Essays in Biblical Theology* (Philadelphia: Fortress, 1986), pp. 68-93.

[55]For some thought-provoking reasons to reconsider Stendahl's conclusions, see J. M. Espy, "Paul's 'Robust Conscience' Re-examined," *NTS* 31 (1985): 161-88. See too C. K. Barrett, "Paul and the Introspective Conscience," in *The Bible, the Reformation and the Church: Festschrift for James Atkinson*, ed. W. P. Stephens (Sheffield: Academic, 1995), pp. 36-48.

[56]Timo Laato, *Paul and Judaism: An Anthropological Approach*, South Florida Studies in the History of Judaism 115, trans. T. McElwain (Atlanta: Scholars Press, 1995). Laato takes his point of departure from a suggestion of Hugh Odeberg, who was professor of New Testament at Lund in the middle of the twentieth century. See Odeberg's *Pharisaism and Christianity* (1943), trans. J. M. Moe (St. Louis: Concordia, 1964), which in a number of ways anticipated much of the recent discussion.

the more optimistic Jewish view, Paul views human nature as dominated by sin and the flesh. Laato notes that Robert Gundry had already come to a similar conclusion about the importance of human weakness for Paul's understanding of salvation.[57] The result is that Paul abandoned the synergism of Jewish soteriology for the monergism of total dependence upon the grace of God in Christ. Laato concludes, rightly in my opinion, that Paul thus repudiates the Jewish understanding of righteousness and the Jewish soteriology. We may compare these conclusions with those of Stephen Westerholm, who also argues that in Paul's view "human sin has rendered the righteous of the law inoperable as a means to life," and who also points out Paul's pessimism, compared to Judaism, in holding the impossibility of human beings ever satisfying the divine requirements.[58]

The question remains concerning when Paul came to this more negative assessment of the human condition.[59] In my view there is some truth in Sanders's argument that Paul moved from solution to problem. I am not convinced that Paul was problem free before the Damascus Road experience, but I am confident that, as Paul began to make sense of the reality of the crucified Messiah as the single *hilasterion* for the forgiveness of sin, his sense of the enormity of the human problem increased dramatically. Although I cannot prove it, I suspect that his experience as a Pharisee had already shown him something of the problem. The law, after all, can be experienced as both a blessing and burden at the same time (as I take Acts 15:10 to indicate). And it is

---

[57]Laato, *Paul and Judaism*, p. 209. Laato quotes these words of Gundry: "It appears that the twin pillars of human weakness and salvation-history, not just salvation-history, uphold justification by faith alone" ("Grace, Works, and Staying Saved in Paul," *Bib 66* [1985]: 27 [1-38]).

[58]Westerholm, *Israel's Law*, p. 142.

[59]In Gundry's view, this question is of no significance, since it does not affect the position Paul takes in his writings; "Grace, Works," p. 21.

impossible to believe that Saul the Pharisee did not know from his own experience what it was like to struggle against the *Yetzer HaRa* (the evil inclination), which is described by C. G. Montefiore as "a sore burden and a heavy trial."[60]

It may well be then that Paul is not so far from Luther as some have recently argued. Instead Luther may indeed have been quite a good exegete of Paul and his theology truly Pauline. Stephen Westerholm's tongue-in-cheek comment at the end of his chapter on justification is apropos: "Students who want to understand Paul but feel they have nothing to learn from a Martin Luther should consider a career in metallurgy."[61]

5.2 In my opinion, *conversion* is the right word to use for Paul's rejection of Judaism and turning to the faith of the Christian community he had been persecuting. But I do *not* think that it is correct to say that he converted to a new religion or that Paul himself would ever have thought so. Christianity, for Paul, is nothing other than the faith of his ancestors come to an eschatological phase of fulfillment before the final consummation. The Christian community is the true Israel, if not the new Israel. The church has for the time being taken the place of Israel, but not altogether, since Paul foresees a future for physical Israel in Romans 11. That future, I hasten to add, involves Israel's response of faith to Jesus Christ. Paul, in my opinion, knows of no salvation—not even for Israel—apart from the cross of Jesus. The church and believing Israel compose one entity, the people of God, who together experience the eschatological goal toward which God's work from Abraham onwards was aimed.[62]

---

[60]Montefiore, *Rabbinic Literature*, p. 180. It is quite probable that Romans 7, if it is autobiographical, reflects something of this agonizing struggle under the law.
[61]Westerholm, *Israel's Law*, p. 173.
[62]See Scott Hafemann, "The Salvation of Israel in Romans 11:25-32: A Response to Krister Stendahl," *Ex Auditu* 4 (1988): 38-58.

Along with his conversion Paul, of course, received a call and commission to evangelize the Gentiles. But, again, Paul did not think of a second religion for the Gentiles. He was calling them to his fulfilled Judaism, nothing other than the faith of Israel beginning with Abraham. For Paul, becoming a Christian did not mean becoming a Gentile; it would be truer to say that the Gentiles became fulfilled Jews, the children of Abraham by faith, grafted onto the olive tree of Israel.

5.3 Paul's gospel addresses not merely the plight of the Gentiles, strangers to the covenants, but that too of the Jews. He addresses a human condition. This I think can be shown by a careful exegetical analysis of Romans 1:18–3:20. The very way Paul has constructed the argument indicates that he means to indict all humanity, both Gentiles and Jews (and the latter despite all their advantages), under the curse of sin (see especially 3:9; 19-20; and further in Romans, 5:18-19). We cannot stop here to look at these and other relevant passages that could be mentioned.

Paul was, of course, concerned especially with the problem of the salvation of the Gentiles, for whom he had been given special responsibility. At the same time, however, he believed his gospel to be universally relevant. In a poignant passage he reveals his concern for the evangelization of the Jews as well as the Gentiles: "For though I am free with respect to all, I have made myself a slave to all, so that I might win more of them. To the Jews I became as a Jew, in order to win Jews. To those under the law I became as one under the law (though I myself am not under the law) so that I might win those under the law" (1 Cor 9:19-20 NRSV). Indeed, the gospel was *first* for the Jews and only subsequently for the Gentiles (Rom 1:16).

This means that Paul had modified the "standard" view of the unconditional election of all Israel, namely its secure place within the covenant promises without qualification. In a recent thorough examination of the Judaism of the Pseudepigrapha and the Dead Sea Scrolls, Mark Adam Elliott has shown that in at least one major strand of Judaism the expectation was that only a remnant of Israel would experience salvation and that judgment would come upon the nation as a whole. Thus a number of New Testament motifs questioned in the recent emphasis on covenantal nomism and the new perspective on Paul are found to have a background within Judaism itself:

> including that Israel, God's chosen people, is in danger of judgment and in this regard has been placed on a par with Gentiles; that the historical covenants are not unqualifiedly valid for all who consider themselves participants in them; that the normal rites of maintaining the covenant have become ineffective; that an individual soteriology *apart from* previous divine acts of deliverance on behalf of Israel has now become necessary.[63]

5.4 The subject of Paul and the law has received much attention lately. It would be impossible to review the discussion here.[64] What I can do is to respond briefly to the claim that Paul

---

[63]Mark Adam Elliott, *The Survivors of Israel: A Reconsideration of the Theology of Pre-Christian Judaism* (Grand Rapids, Mich.: Eerdmans, 2000), p. 664.

[64]At least the following significant monographs may be listed: Hans Hübner, *Law in Paul's Thought* (1978), trans. James C. G. Greig (Edinburgh: T & T Clark, 1984); Räisänen, *Paul and the Law*; Sanders, *Paul, the Law, and the Jewish People*; Brice L. Martin, *Christ and the Law in Paul*, NovTSup 62 (Leiden: Brill, 1989); Frank Thielman, *From Plight to Solution: A Jewish Framework for Understanding Paul's View of the Law in Galatians and Romans*, NovTSup 61 (Leiden: Brill, 1989); Tomson, *Paul and the Jewish Law*; Dunn, *Jesus, Paul and the Law*; Michael Winger, *By What Law? The Meaning of Nomos in the Letters of Paul*, SBLDS 128 (Atlanta: Scholars Press, 1992); Schreiner, *Law and Its Fulfillment*; Frank Thielman, *Paul and the Law: A Contextual Approach* (Downers Grove, Ill.: InterVarsity Press, 1994); Kruse, *Paul, the Law and Justification*; and especially the essays from the third Durham-Tübingen Symposium on Earliest Christianity and Judaism edited by Dunn, *Paul and the Mosaic Law*. For useful and contrasting reviews of scholarship in this area, see Douglas J. Moo, "Paul and the Law in the Last Ten Years," *SJT* 40 (1987): 287-307; A. J. M. Wedderburn, "Paul and the

has no quarrel with the law.[65] Some preliminary comments will lead us quickly to the question of "works of the law," which will require a little more detailed treatment.

Recent discussion of the subject shows its complexity. My conviction is that we must learn to tolerate the paradox. That is, Paul both does away with and upholds the law—in different senses, of course, unless we are to accept Heikki Räisänen's desperate conclusion that Paul was simply very confused.[66] But is Paul's dialectic on this subject really so hard to understand? The assertion that the law has come to an end (e.g., Rom 7:4-6; Gal 3:23-25; 4:4-5) is fundamentally important for Paul's soteriology (note the first person pronoun in Gal 2:4; cf. 2:15-16), this in the first instance in response to what de facto legalism may have existed, but also in response even to an authentic covenantal nomism. Paradoxically, however, those free from the law who follow the teaching of their Lord fulfill the righteousness of the law apart from the law—that is, they fulfill the moral law, espe-

Law," *SJT* 38 (1985): 613-22; J. M. G. Barclay, "Paul and the Law: Observations on Some Recent Debates," *Themelios* 12 (1986): 5-15; F. F. Bruce, "Paul and the Law in Recent Research," in *Law and Religion: Essays on the Place of the Law in Israel and Early Christianity*, ed. Barnabas Lindars (Cambridge: James Clarke, 1988), pp. 115-25; and A. J. Bandstra, "Paul and the Law: Some Recent Developments and an Extraordinary Book," *CTJ* 25 (1990): 249-61. Also worth mentioning is Seyoon Kim, "Postscript to the Second Edition," in *The Origin of Paul's Gospel* (Tübingen: Mohr, 1984), where Räisänen and, to a lesser extent, Sanders are sharply criticized (pp. 345-58). Kim's views are expounded more fully in *Paul and the New Perspective: Second Thoughts on the Origin of Paul's Gospel* (Grand Rapids, Mich.: Eerdmans, 2001).

[65]For full treatment of the question, see Donald A. Hagner, "Paul's Quarrel with Judaism," in *Anti-Semitism and Early Christianity. Issues of Polemic and Faith*, ed. Craig A. Evans and Donald A. Hagner (Minneapolis: Fortress, 1993), pp. 128-50.

[66]Räisänen, *Paul and the Law*, e.g., p. 264: "He [Paul] is torn into [sic] two directions, and he is incapable of resolving the tension in terms of theological thought." There have been many responses to Räisänen's book. He responds to these (up to 1987) in the preface to the second edition of his book. See further now G. Klein, "Ein Sturmzentrum der Paulusforschung," *Verkündigung und Forschung* 33 (1988): 40-56; and C. E. B. Cranfield, "Giving a Dog a Bad Name: A Note on H. Räisänen's *Paul and the Law*," *JSNT* 38 (1990): 77-85.

cially as summarized in the love commandment (Rom 13:9-10; cf. Mt 22:37-40). Thus it can be said that the gospel does not overthrow the law in the sense that righteousness is abandoned; rather, the gospel upholds the ultimate intention of the law (Rom 3:31).[67] As I see it, the telos of Romans 10:4 may itself thus bear both the nuance of "end" and "goal." Both are surely true from the Pauline viewpoint.

If Paul in this sense still upholds the law, may it not be said that his Christianity amounts simply to a variant form of "covenantal nomism"? Is it not a following of the law in the context of experienced grace? Several scholars have noted the duality of covenant grace and meritorious works in Judaism, and have found a similar synergism in Paul. Mikael Winninge can speak of justification in Paul as a "continual participation, where God and the Christian 'cooperate' in a progressive dialectic," in which God by grace confers righteous status (cf. Israel's election) and the Christian produces the necessary works that determine reward or punishment.[68] Very similar is Kent Yinger's conclusion that as in Judaism, so in Pauline Christianity, despite differences, "the fundamental structure of grace and works, election and obedience, salvation and judgment, remains the same."[69] Hendrikus Boers takes almost exactly the same line, stressing that Paul the Christian remained

---

[67]For a somewhat similar perspective, see Peter Stuhlmacher, "Paul's Understanding of the Law in the Letter to the Romans," SEÅ 50 (1985): 87-104; and also his Reconciliation, Law, and Righteousness, pp. 134-54. See also D. A. Hagner, "Balancing the Old and the New: The Law of Moses in Matthew and Paul," Int 51 (1997): 20-30.

[68]Mikael Winninge, Sinners and the Righteous: A Comparative Study of the Psalms of Solomon and Paul's Letters, ConBNT 26 (Stockholm: Almqvist & Wiksell, 1995), p. 334. Winninge denies that his view involves a legalism or Pelagianism since righteous status is a divine gift.

[69]Kent Yinger, Paul, Judaism, and Judgment According to Deeds, SNTSMS 105 (Cambridge: Cambridge University Press, 1999). Yinger says that for Paul the Jew there was no theological tension between judgment according to works and justification by faith. But if Paul saw no problem with works-righteousness, why did he repeatedly argue so strongly against it?

Jewish in his valuation of the law and the necessity of works of the law, and that "in many ways he can be understood better as a Jewish sectarian (in the sense of Acts 24:14) than as a Christian."[70]

While there is indeed some overt similarity between the soteriology of Paul and that of Judaism, the very basis of Paul's soteriology is different. I can do no better than quote Morna Hooker here:

> Clearly we cannot speak of "covenantal nomism" in Paul's case, since that would run counter to Paul's basic quarrel with the Law. But the point is that for Paul, the Law has been replaced by Christ—or rather, since the Law was an interim measure, it has been shown in its true character as a stand-in, now that the reality has arrived. The questions, "Who belongs to the covenant?", and "How does one respond to the covenant?", are answered by Paul in terms of Christ, by Judaism in terms of the Law.[71]

 In short, while Judaism is nomocentric, Paul is christocentric. And as serious as Paul is about righteous conduct, he cannot be fairly characterized as a nomist (cf. Gal 3:1-5). He has in a fundamental way broken with the law[72] and hence with Judaism.[73]

---

[70]Hendrikus Boers, "Judaism and the Church in Paul's Thought," *Neotestamentica* 32 (1998): 249-66. Boers differs markedly from Yinger, however, in detecting not merely tensions in Paul's theology, but contradictions, à la Räisänen: "These contradictions constitute one of the most fundamental problems in the interpretation of Paul. The question can no longer be *whether* Paul makes contradictory statements, but *how it was possible* for him to do so" (p. 256).

[71]Morna Hooker, "Paul and 'Covenantal Nomism'," in *Paul and Paulinism, Festschrift for C. K. Barrett,* ed. M. D. Hooker and S. G. Wilson (London: SPCK, 1982), p. 52 (47-56). Hooker has more than once been quoted as though she equated Paul's Christianity with a covenantal nomism.

[72]So rightly Räisänen, who notes, "The real difference between Dunn and me (and Sanders) is not the assessment of the social function of the law but the question of whether or not Paul criticized the *law as such and as a whole* or just the law as viewed from a limited perspective" *(Paul and the Law,* p. xxx). For a particularly strong statement concerning Paul's rejection of the law, see Robert G. Hamerton-Kelly, "Sacred Violence and 'Works of Law': 'Is Christ Then an Agent of Sin?' (Galatians 2:17)," *CBQ* 52 (1990): 55-75. See also his *Sacred Violence: Paul's Hermeneutic of the Cross* (Minneapolis: Fortress, 1992).

[73]See especially Heikki Räisänen, "Galatians 2.16 and Paul's Break with Juda-

5.5 That brings us finally to the vexed question of the meaning of "works of the law" in Paul. The attempt to avoid a negation of the law on Paul's part makes necessary a reunderstanding of this phrase as referring to something other than the performance of the law itself. Already in 1975 Daniel P. Fuller, in pursuit of the unity of the Testaments, argued that "works of the law" referred to a legalistic distortion of the law on the part of the Judaizers.[74] The recent attempts of a number of scholars to understand the phrase as referring to "boundary markers" or the specific indicators of Jewish distinctiveness have essentially the same motivation. This is indeed a key element in the new perspective on Paul as defended particularly by Dunn.

This understanding of "works of the law" has not been without its share of critics. In the informative "Additional Notes" to the relevant chapters (eight and nine), Dunn responds in turn to the criticisms of Räisänen, Hübner, Stuhlmacher, Sanders, Bruce, Schreiner, Fung and Westerholm.[75] More recently, in a separate article, he responds to the criticisms of C. E. B. Cranfield.[76] It is impossible here to review these discussions in any detail. All I can do is note a couple of common motifs in the objections and make a few additional observations.

It is a frequent, and to my mind justifiable, objection among these writers that in Paul's soteriological arguments works of the law and gospel are antithetical and that one aspect of the good news of the gospel is that it involves a break with the law and hence that Paul's Christianity includes a break with Judaism. This, of course, amounts to a denial of the new perspective at its

---

ism," NTS 31 (1985): 543-53.

[74]Daniel P. Fuller, "Paul and 'The Works of the Law,' " WTJ 38 (1975-1976): 28-42.

[75]See Dunn, Jesus, Paul and the Law, pp. 206-14; 237-41.

[76]C. E. B. Cranfield, "'The Works of the Law' in the Epistle to the Romans," JSNT 43 (1991): 89-101; James D. G. Dunn, "Yet Once More—'The Works of the Law': A Response," JSNT 46 (1992): 99-117.

very center. A further point is that Paul's argument is not simply against the so-called boundary markers but refers to the entirety of the law (a point admitted by Dunn). Dunn consistently faults his critics for failing to appreciate the social function of the law, by which he appears to mean failing to explain "works of the law" solely in terms of social boundary markers.

Now it can hardly be denied that Dunn's fundamental point is true. The law does play a socially determinative role in its boundary markers separating Jew from Gentile, and Paul would have used all resources at his disposal to argue against wrong soteriological inferences from this.[77] But the fact that there was such a social aspect involving such boundary markers does not warrant reducing the entirety of Paul's polemic against the law to this one single point. Precisely because the law was what distinguished the Jew from the Gentile, the boasting that Paul attacks can be explained as boasting in national privileges. That, however, is not a necessary explanation of the relevant Pauline texts; it remains possible that Paul attacks a legalistic boasting. Gundry's conclusion is correct: "The use of the law to establish one's own righteousness is what Paul finds wrong in Palestinian Judaism, including his past life."[78]

---

[77]I do not see that a full admission of this point can help bring the two sides together (the old and new perspectives on Paul) into some kind of blend, as the irenically minded Bruce Longenecker would have it, nor do I understand why Longenecker describes himself as an advocate of the new perspective when he seems to accept the essentials of the so-called Lutheran understanding of Paul and the law. See Longenecker's *The Triumph of Abraham's God: The Transformation of Identity in Galatians* (Edinburgh: T & T Clark, 1998), pp. 76-77; 179-83; and "Lifelines: Perspectives on Paul and the Law," *Anvil* 1 (1999): 125-30. Note especially his statement that there are Pauline passages (e.g., Rom 4:4-5; 9:32; 11:5-6) "where Paul does seem to suggest that nomistic observance can be a form of legalism" ("Contours of Covenant Theology in the Post-Conversion Paul," in *The Road from Damascus: The Impact of Paul's Conversion on His Life, Thought, and Ministry*, ed. Richard N. Longenecker [Grand Rapids, Mich.: Eerdmans, 1997], p. 140 [125-46]).
[78]Gundry, "Grace, Works," p. 16. At the end of his article Gundry states that it was "because of a conviction that works-righteousness lay at the heart of Judaism and Judaistic Christianity" that Paul rejected them (pp. 37-38).

For all its undeniable truth, one may wonder whether the view of works of the law as badges of national identity really provides the best explanation of all the data.[79]

---

[79]In addition to the literature mentioned above in note 64, among the ever-burgeoning literature on the subject the following may also be noted: E. P. Sanders, "On the Question of Fulfilling the Law in Paul and Rabbinic Judaism," in *Donum Gentilicium: Festschrift for David Daube*, ed. E. Bammel, C. K. Barrett, and W. D. Davies (Oxford: Clarendon, 1978), pp. 103-26; (R. Smend) and Ulrich Luz, *Gesetz* (Stuttgart: Kohlhammer, 1981), pp. 45-144. The following three articles appear in the same volume: W. D. Davies, "Paul and the Law: Reflections on Pitfalls in Interpretation," pp. 4-16; U. Wilckens, "Statements on the Development of Paul's View of the Law," pp. 17-26; and F. F. Bruce, "The Curse of the Law," pp. 27-36, *Paul and Paulinism: Festschrift for C. K. Barrett*, ed. M. D. Hooker and S. G. Wilson (London: SPCK, 1982). Douglas J. Moo, "'Law,' 'Works of the Law,' and Legalism in Paul," *WTJ* 45 (1983): 73-100; N. M. Watson, "Justified by Faith, Judged by Works—An Antinomy?" *NTS* 29 (1983): 209-21; Thomas R. Schreiner, "Is Perfect Obedience to the Law Possible? A Re-examination of Galatians 3:10," *JETS* 27 (1984): 151-60; "Paul and Perfect Obedience to the Law: An Evaluation of the View of E. P. Sanders," *WTJ* 47 (1985): 245-78; B. Reicke, "Paulus über das Gesetz," *ThZ* 41 (1985): 237-57; Stuhlmacher, "Paul's Understanding"; Hans Hübner, "Was heißt bei Paulus 'Werke des Gesetzes'?" *Glaube und Eschatologie: Festschrift for Werner George Kummel*, ed. Erich Gräßer and Otto Merk (Tübingen: Mohr, 1985), pp. 123-33; Heikki Räisänen, *The Torah and Christ: Essays in German and English on the Problem of the Law in Early Christianity* (Helsinki: Finnish Exegetical Society, 1986); Terrence L. Donaldson, "The 'Curse of the Law' and the Inclusion of the Gentiles: Galatians 3.13-14," *NTS* 32 (1986): 94-112; J. Lambrecht, "Gesetzesverständnis bei Paulus," in *Das Gesetz im Neuen Testament*, ed. Karl Kertelge (Freiburg: Herder, 1986), pp. 88-127; Snodgrass, "Justification by Grace"; Charles H. Cosgrove, "Justification in Paul: A Linguistic and Theological Reflection," *JBL* 106 (1987): 653-70; T. D. Gordon, "The Problem at Galatia," *Int* 41 (1987): 32-43; Klyne R. Snodgrass, "Spheres of Influence: A Possible Solution to the Problem of Paul and the Law," *JSNT* 32 (1988): 93-113; Brice L. Martin, *Christ and the Law in Paul*, NovTSup 62 (Leiden: Brill, 1989); Thielman, *From Plight;* Terrence L. Donaldson, "Zealot and Convert: The Origin of Paul's Christ-Torah Antithesis," *CBQ* 51 (1989): 655-82; Thomas R. Schreiner, "The Abolition and Fulfillment of the Law in Paul," *JSNT* 35 (1989): 47-74; Robert G. Hamerton-Kelly, "Sacred Violence and 'Works of Law': Is Christ Then an Agent of Sin?' (Galatians 2:17)," *CBQ* 52 (1990): 55-75; Christopher D. Stanley, "'Under a Curse': A Fresh Reading of Galatians 3.10-14," *NTS* 36 (1990): 481-511; Jeffrey A. D. Weima, "The Function of the Law in Relation to Sin: An Evaluation of the View of H. Räisänen," *NovT* 32 (1990): 219-35; Peter Richardson, Stephen Westerholm et al., *Law in Religious Communities in the Roman Period: The Debate Over Torah and Nomos in Post-Biblical Judaism and Early Christianity*, Studies in Christianity and Judaism 4 (Waterloo, Ontario: Wilfrid Laurier University Press, 1991); Don B. Garlington, "The Obedience of Faith": A Pauline Phrase in Historical

5.6 This is not the place to argue against the two-covenant theory concerning the salvation of the Jews and the Gentiles.[80] As noted earlier, not all advocates of the newer approach to Paul hold to this view. Here I refer only to a significant article by Sanders in which, critiquing the views of Stendahl, he argues that, according to Paul, Torah obedience is not "the necessary or sufficient condition of salvation" for Israel, and that when Paul envisages the salvation of Israel, he has no other way in mind than "the requirement of faith in Christ."[81] Sanders himself dissents from this viewpoint, but he is fair enough to indicate what Paul's view was. For Paul, Christ was not merely one event in a series of salvation-historical events.[82]

Context, WUNT 2.38 (Tübingen: Mohr Siebeck, 1991); "The Obedience of Faith in the Letter to the Romans," *WTJ* 52 (1990): 201-24, and 53 (1991): 47-52; J. P. Braswell, " 'The Blessing of Abraham' Versus 'The Curse of the Law': Another Look at Gal 3:10-13," *WTJ* 53 (1991): 73-91; Schreiner, " 'Works of Law' in Paul"; Robert B. Sloan, "Paul and the Law: Why the Law Cannot Save," *NovT* 33 (1991): 35-60; Hermann Lichtenberger, "Paulus und das Gesetz," *Paulus und das antike Judentum*, WUNT 58 (Tübingen: Mohr Siebeck, 1991), pp. 361-78; James D. G. Dunn, "What Was the Issue Between Paul and 'Those of the Circumcision'?", WUNT 58 (Tübingen: Mohr Siebeck, 1991), pp. 295-318; N. T. Wright, *The Climax of the Covenant: Christ and the Law in Pauline Theology* (Minneapolis: Fortress, 1992); H. Boers, " 'We Who Are by Inheritance Jews; Not from the Gentiles, Sinners,' " *JBL* 111 (1992): 273-81; Frank Thielman, "The Coherence of Paul's View of the Law," *NTS* 38 (1992): 235-53; J. M. Scott, " 'For As Many As Are of Works of the Law Are Under a Curse' (Galatians 3.10)," in *Paul and the Scriptures of Israel*, ed. Craig A. Evans and James A. Sanders, SSEJC 1 (Sheffield: Academic, 1993), pp. 187-221; *Paul and the Mosaic Law*, ed. James D. G. Dunn (Tübingen: Mohr Siebeck, 1996; Grand Rapids, Mich.: Eerdmans, 2001).
[80]See Kai Kjær-Hansen, "The Problem of the Two-Covenant Theology," *Mishkan* 21 (1994): 52-81.
[81]"Paul's Attitude Toward the Jewish People," *USQR* 33 (1978): 184 (175-87). The article is followed by "A Response" from Krister Stendahl, pp. 189-91. See especially the excellent articles of Reidar Hvalvik, "A 'Sonderweg' for Israel: A Critical Examination of a Current Interpretation of Romans 11, 25-27," *JSNT* 38 (1990): 87-107; and Scott Hafemann, "The Salvation of Israel in Romans 11:25-32: A Response to Krister Stendahl," *Ex Auditu* 4 (1988): 38-58.
[82]Compare D. C. Allison Jr.: "The NT nowhere holds that salvation is to be found apart from Jesus, the Messiah and Son of God. Although this may ride roughshod over our modern sensibilities, it remains no less true. The NT does not know two ways of salvation—one in Jesus, one apart from him" ("Jesus and the

Those who agree with Paul here, I hasten to add, must oppose anti-Semitism with all the strength available to them.

6. The ultimate test of the new perspective on Paul is how well it can explain all the pertinent texts. Proponents of the new perspective, like those of the old perspective (if we may call it that), must not only occupy themselves with texts that seem to support their views but also explain those that seem to go against them.[83] Those who are unconvinced by the new perspective must be able to handle such texts as Romans 2:6-10, 13-16; 3:31; 8:3-4. Supporters of the new perspective have to explain such texts as Romans 3:20, 28; 4:4-6; 5:20; 11:6; and Galatians 2:16; 3:10-14, and convince us that "works of the law" in every case refers only to boundary markers and the social function of the law. Dunn has, of course, addressed these texts in his various articles, his Romans and Galatians commentaries, and in the exchange with Cranfield referred to above.[84] It will naturally be a matter of opinion as to which view in the end does the best justice to the texts. The discussion seems destined to go on for yet some time.

Covenant: A Response to E. P. Sanders," *JSNT* 29 [1987]: 74 [57-78]). See too Räisänen, *Paul and the Law*, p. xxiv.

[83]Silva calls for a closer examination of a number of texts by Dunn, adding that "no explanation of Paul's theology can prove ultimately persuasive if it does not arise from the very heart of Paul's explicit affirmations and denials" ("Law and Christianity," p. 353).

[84]Dunn summarizes his differences with Cranfield as centering on two key issues: (1) "Did Paul accuse his fellow Jews of seeking to earn salvation by works of the law, or of seeking to preserve their covenantal privileges as God's righteous ones (over against Gentile sinners) by works of the law?" and (2) "Did Paul think the law could not be obeyed and that Israel's fault was in assuming that it could? Or did he think that Israel was going about obeying the law in the wrong way, by treating the realm of righteousness as exclusively Jewish territory (marked out by works of the law), and thereby failing to recognize the seriousness of their sin and that they (as much as any Gentile) fell under the law's curse?" In both instances, Cranfield opts for the first alternative, Dunn for the second (cf. "Yet Once More—'The Works of the Law,'" p. 116).

7. The new perspective on Paul has been effectively argued by its most able proponent, James D. G. Dunn. Taking the groundwork laid by Sanders and giving full due to the social situation of the early church, Dunn has been able to provide a remarkably cohesive explanation of the texts in which Paul addresses the issue of the law. It cannot reasonably be in question that Paul disapproved of viewing the law as a boundary marker of Jewish righteousness over against the Gentiles. Paul does do away with Jewish privileges and the Jewish-Gentile distinction so far as salvation is concerned. This was clearly of supreme importance to the success of the Gentile mission to which he had been called. It is precisely because this is important in the Pauline texts that Dunn's case can be as strong as it is. Many of us continue to wonder, however, whether this is *all* Paul fights against in his polemic against the law and whether the improper "boasting" he opposes does not involve something else equally serious, if not more so. In some of us there lingers the feeling that in a number of instances Paul seems to have picked a strange way of arguing—a way that must be regarded as indirect and misleading—if he is concerned *solely* about the national distinctives and privileges of Israel, and nothing more.

To be fair to Dunn, he does state unequivocally that his main contention concerning boundary markers does not cancel out the importance of the Protestant doctrine of justification by faith.[85] My impression, however, is that the emphasis on boundary markers or national righteousness, in fact, pushes justifica-

---

[85]See, for example, Dunn, "Justice of God," pp. 2, 21. I do not understand Dunn's praise of the Reformation doctrine of justification by faith as "a restatement of central biblical insights of incalculable influence and priceless value" (p. 2), when his approach explains the pertinent passages in a quite different way. I also find it difficult to understand J. A. Ziesler's claim that justification by faith can be preserved in the new perspective as an analogy. See "Justification by Faith in the Light of the 'New Perspective' on Paul," *Theology* 94 (1991): 188-94.

tion by faith very much to the periphery, making it pertinent only to the Gentiles. The problem is a bigger one than simply holding the two emphases in balance. Despite Dunn's claim, I do not see how his approach can do anything but take all vitality out of the doctrine.

That some valid insights have emerged in the new perspective on Paul, I do not wish to deny. I find myself doubtful, however, that the new perspective itself constitutes a major breakthrough to a truer estimate of Paul and Judaism. This Copernican revolution is taking us down the wrong path.